Omar A. Ayaita

AF209215

Philosophical Knowledge

The Search for Truth and its Limits

Printed by Books on Demand, Norderstedt (Germany), in 2010.
ISBN 978-3-8391-8789-0

Contents

Preface

This little book is aimed at a slightly better understanding of certain philosophical topics that are related to truth and knowledge. Arguments, formal logic and thought experiments will be used to argue for the following theses:

- If a statement makes sense at all, then it is either true or false. Relativism is not plausible.
- Nevertheless, we often do not know *which* sentences are true and which are false.
- But knowledge is possible; the thesis that we do not know anything is exaggerated.
- What, for example, do we know in philosophy? There are some candidates for philosophical knowledge; that is, there are some philosophical positions that we have good reasons to believe in, and that are presumably true.
- The plausible philosophical theses include: Human minds are completely material. Psychology can nevertheless not be reduced to physics.
- The truth of some other philosophical theses is more doubtful: Our knowledge about Free Will and the existence or non-existence of God is extremely limited, because the definition of important terms is particularly controversial in these topics.

Most parts of the book should be easy to understand. However, some basic knowledge in theoretical philosophy and logic may be useful to understand some of the details.

During the last years, I studied different subjects – but mainly philosophy – at three universities, which were equally important for the development of my ideas: the University of Tübingen, the University of Konstanz (both in Germany) and the University of Massachusetts Amherst (USA). Some of the books and papers that I read in college were nearly irrelevant for my main intellectual interests; but others were of much importance for me and for this book. Some of these relevant writings are mentioned in my book and listed in the bibliography.

This book looks like a monograph, but it is indeed the result of much team work. My interest for philosophy started in high school, and if I had not attended Latin and Ancient Greek courses, then this book would never have been written. My special thanks go to my former high school teachers Gerhard Fiedler and Irene Polke.[1]

Among my college teachers, who were particularly important because they showed and gave me a lot of relevant literature, I want to thank these: Frank Hofmann, Andreas Schmidt, Otfried Höffe, Fred Feldman, Peter Graham, Gary Hardegree and Hilary Kornblith.

Some teachers in high school and college nominated me for scholarships, which were of much importance for my intellectual life. Without the *Studienstiftung des deutschen Volkes*, the *Baden-Württemberg Stipendium* and the Fulbright Commission, it would have been impossible or much more difficult to study independently and in different cities, not to mention

---

[1] I apologize for not mentioning any academic titles throughout the book.

other advantages that I took of summer seminars and the like.

In the *Leibniz Kolleg*, an institution in Tübingen that is led by Michael Behal, I met a lot of people who I had important discussions with. Discussions with Sebastian Ulrich were particularly important for some chapters of the book.

I thank the *Forum Scientiarum* in Tübingen, led by Niels Weidtmann and Dirk Evers, where I got some insight into important empirical findings concerning the human mind.

I also want to thank Doris Ayaita; without her help it would not have been possible to spend this interesting year in the United States.

My crucial motivation for writing this little book was the wish to create something that will survive, even when I do not. The summer of 2010 turned out to be a good opportunity to fulfill this wish. Furthermore, it seemed to me that some of the things that are said in academic discourse and every-day life are rather confused, so that it would be interesting to clarify those issues.

The reader should not read every part of this book; there are more interesting things to do. But he can treat the book as a supermarket, a collection of things that have different values, and just pick those ideas and arguments that are important for him.

Truth, knowledge, religion: Someone might wonder why I try to write on so many hard issues in such a small book. First of all, I do not write a full explanation (whatever this may be) of all these phenomena. I focus on particular aspects and give some arguments. Some of these arguments are not new, but important and sometimes neglected; others are based on some new literature, and some are invented by me. Furthermore, most problems in this book are surprisingly easy. This is the reason why a guy like me can write on them.

At the very end of this preface, I want to apologize for my bad English. I wished English were my native language, or that I were as good as a native speaker. Obviously, neither is the case.

Omar A. Ayaita   Fuldatal, June 2010

Part I: On Truth and Knowledge in general

1   On Truth

1.1   Introduction

Some people think that there are different points of view and that something can be true from one perspective but false from another perspective – that some statements are neither absolutely true nor absolutely false, or both true and false, dependent on the perspective. This position can be called 'relativism'. Joseph Ratzinger described how some current relativists think. Nowadays, he observed, truth is regarded as something that can only be private and that can never be objective (public):

> "The notion of truth has been moved towards intolerance and against democracy. Truth is not a public, but only a private thing or something for a group, but not for the whole. In other words: The modern notion of democracy seems to be inevitably connected with relativism; and relativism seems to be the real guaranty for freedom, especially for its essential core – the freedom of religion and conscious." (Ratzinger 2005: 51; my translation)

Ratzinger criticizes this position. In contrast, he suggests that relativism destroys freedom in the long run. (cf. especially 57 et seq.) Here I am not concerned with the plausibility or implausibility of his own position. But I assume that his observation concerning current relativism that I quoted above is adequate. Motivated by this description, we can take a step towards theoretical philosophy and define 'relativism' this way:

> **Relativism** =df. Some propositions do not have an absolute truth value. That is: There are some propositions that are either both true and false or neither true nor false.

Before I go on with a discussion of relativism, I should give a rough definition of the term 'proposition'. In this book, I use the term 'proposition' nearly identical as the term 'sentence', but not exactly identical. To use a standard example: 'Schnee ist weiß' and 'Snow is white' are two different sentences (for the simple reason that one is a German sentence and the other one is an English sentence). But both sentences express the same proposition: the proposition that snow is white. Propositions are what sentences assert. If and only if two sentences assert the same state of affairs, then they express the same proposition. The sentences 'Obama is sitting in the White House' and 'The current president of the United States is sitting in the White House' assert the same state of affairs, because Obama is identical to the current president of the United States; therefore, both sentences express the same proposition.[2]

---

[2] To say that propositions are what sentences assert, may be a simplification. See Frank Hofmann (2008), where he says "Propositions cannot simply be equated with meanings of sen-

Note, furthermore, that not every sentence expresses a proposition. The sentence 'Please bring coffee, Steven!' does not express any proposition, because this sentence does not assert anything; it is a request, not an assertion. And the sentence 'What is the time?' does not express a proposition either, because it asks something instead of asserting something. What about this sentence: 'Marilyn Monroe is identical to hugcernabble.' This sentence does not make any sense. You could, therefore, either say that this sentence expresses a proposition that is non-sense (or without sense, or not significant); or you could simply say that the sentence does not express any proposition at all. These rough explanations should be enough for our purposes here.

The definition of relativism that I gave above contains the word 'truth value'. A truth value is the truth or falsity of a proposition. The proposition 'There are currently more than three books in Vienna' is true; this is the same as to say that the truth value of this proposition is 'true'. The proposition 'There are currently more than three people on the moon' has the truth value 'false'. To say that every proposition has a truth value is the same as to say that every proposition is either true or false. Relativists deny that. The question that this chapter deals with is the question whether relativism is plausible. The answer is No.

---

tences" (27; my translation). But it does not seem that this simplification is problematic in our context.

1.2 Reasons for Relativism

These propositions do not seem to have an absolute truth value:

[1] Kosovo is a state.

[2] It would be morally right if everybody in the United States got more than 1.000 dollars per month.

[3] Schroedinger's cat is dead at a certain time $t1$.

Is Kosovo a state? Some recognize it as a state, some do not. I do not know enough about the topic, but it seems that there is no absolute answer to the question whether Kosovo is a state. (If this is a bad example, then you may choose another one.) The problem with the truth value of 'Kosovo is a state' can, I think, not be solved by a more detailed definition of the word 'state'. Even if all the countries of the world were sitting together and had decided which definition they want to use, it is still probable that some will say "Yes, Kosovo is a state according to just this definition", while others would reject that. And it may be that neither of them is absolutely right. If this is true, then proposition [1] shows that relativism is true.

Proposition [2] looks very different, because it consists of a moral judgment, but I think that the principle is the same. Some people think that it would be morally right if everybody in the United States got more than 1.000 dollars per month; others think that this would not be right. (Still others would not make a decision or first want to talk about the details of the plan.) I am not sure whether one certain position according to this problem is absolutely true. It is not implausible that there is no absolutely true answer to the question whether it is morally right that everybody gets more than 1.000 dollars. And this problem can, I guess, not be solved by a *definition* of moral rightness; the question is not what 'moral rightness' *means*, but whether a certain type of action *is* morally right or not.[3] If proposition [2] does not have an absolute truth value, then relativism is true.

Proposition [3] refers to a phenomenon in physics. According to some interpretation of quantum mechanics, some properties of particles on micro-level (electrons, protons, etc.) are not determined. For example, some think that an electron is not at one certain position at one certain time. And, perhaps less controversially, the *decay of radioactive material* is one case where indeterminacy occurs: It seems that at a certain time the material has neither decayed nor not decayed (or it has decayed as well as not decayed). Erwin Schroedinger's thought experiment states that a cat is in a box, and there is a mechanism that will kill her exactly when the material has decayed. But because at a certain time (*t1*) the material has decayed *and* not decayed, the cat is dead *and* not dead at *t1*. This example shows how quantum mechanical phenomena can have effects on the macro-level, at least according to some interpretation. If this is true, then propo-

---

[3] The 1.000 dollar example is perhaps a bad example. Because there are arguments for the claim that moral evaluation can only apply to act tokens; whereas 'Everybody gets 1.000 dollars', as I understand it, is neither an act token nor an act at all. But it will not be difficult for the reader to find better examples.

sition [3] does not have an absolute truth value, and relativism is true.[4]

1.3 Against Relativism

It is clear that some propositions do have an absolute truth value. For example:

[4] The holocaust happened.

This is an absolutely true statement, and to deny that the truth of [4] is objective, would be unacceptable. So relativism has a hybrid structure: It has to accept that some propositions do have an absolute truth value, while it also wants to claim that some other propositions do not have an absolute truth value. This hybrid structure is problematic.

A relativist should explain *why* some propositions have an absolute truth value and others not; what is the criterion that decides about a proposition's having or not having an absolute truth value? The relativist could say that moral judgments – and only moral judgments – do not have an absolute truth value. But this is implausible. We want to admit that some moral principles are absolutely true, such as:

[5] It is morally wrong to punish women because they have been raped.

---

[4] What I write about quantum mechanics is based on Diezemann (2006) and Deutsch (1996). I thank Youness Ayaita, who called my attention to the Deutsch paper.

(It has been said to me that in some countries, women are punished by the administration when they have been raped, because their having been raped is interpreted as their own mistake, and as betrayal. This should be regarded as unacceptable, and no relativism is possible in this case.)

The relativist could say that the truth of [4] and [5] is *obvious*; and that in other, less obvious cases, there is no absolute truth value. But why should there be a correlation between the fact how obvious or how accepted the truth value of a proposition is and the fact whether this proposition *has* any absolute truth value? Look at this proposition:

$$\{ \exists x \forall y \, (\, Fy \leftrightarrow y = x \,) \} \leftrightarrow \{ \exists x \, \{ \, Fx \, \& \, \forall y \, (\, Fy \rightarrow y = x \,) \} \}$$

This proposition is absolutely true, as can be shown with identity logic.[5] But is it *obvious* whether the proposition is true? For most people not. Is it widely accepted? Only among some academics. So it does not seem that the question whether a proposition has an absolute truth value is related to the question whether the truth value is obvious. Sometimes the truth is not obvious, and not widely accepted either, but nevertheless absolute. It seems that the relativist cannot explain which propositions do not have an absolute truth value, and why.

Besides this problem, there is a further, logical problem that relativism faces. I will use the rest of this section 1.3 to explain the logical problem to those of us who are interested in formal logic.

---

[5] The proof can be found in Hardegree (2010: 9 et seq.).

If relativism is true, then sentential logic 'breaks down'. If there is one proposition that is both true and false (or neither true nor false), then every proposition can be shown to be true! This can be demonstrated by this logical derivation:

(1) Assumption: p & $\sim p$
(2) p
(3) $p \vee q$
(4) $\sim p$
(5) q

(I found out that such a proof has already been published several times: for example – in a way that looks pretty different from mine – by Karl R. Popper in 1934/1994: p. 58, footnote 2.[6])

According to sentential logic, this is true of every pair of propositions p and q. Let us assume that p is not identical to q. And let us assume that p means 'Kosovo is a state'. Therefore, the assumption (1) is just the assumption that the Kosovo case is a case of a proposition that does not have an absolute truth value: Assumption (1) states that 'Kosovo is a state, and Kosovo is not a state'. From this it follows that the moon consists of ice cream! Because q can be any proposition, and q follows with necessity from (p & $\sim p$).

---

[6] Popper not only offers a different derivation, but he also uses other logical symbols than I do. Using the symbols that I use in this book, his derivation can be written down this way:
(1) $p \rightarrow (p \vee q)$ (this is a logical truth)
(2) $\sim p \rightarrow (\sim p \vee q)$ (this is also a logical truth)
(3) $\sim p \rightarrow (p \rightarrow q)$ (this follows logically from 2)
(4) $(\sim p$ & $p) \rightarrow q$ (this follows logically from 3).

Let q be 'The moon consists of ice cream'. In line (2) we say that Kosovo is a state; that is a simple consequence from the assumption 'Kosovo is a state, and Kosovo is not a state'. Since we know that p, we can state $(p \lor q)$, that is, $(p$ or $q)$. This is generally possible: If you know that 'Grass is green', then you can state that 'Grass is green, or my name is Otto', even if your name is certainly not Otto. So we can state that 'Kosovo is a state, or the moon consists of ice cream' (line 3). But in (1), we also said that Kosovo is *not* a state. We repeat this part of the assumption in line (4). Now, look at (3) and (4) together: line (3) says that at least one of the propositions 'Kosovo is a state' and 'The moon consists of ice cream' is true. Since we derived that Kosovo is *not* a state (line 4), it follows that the moon consists of ice cream (5). This consequence is incredible; the assumption has to be rejected. This means, relativism has to be rejected generally, as long as we believe in sentential logic. Otherwise every proposition, even the most incredible one, can be shown to be true.

But if there cannot be any proposition that is both true and false: How can we, then, deal with the problem of Schroedinger's cat, and – if this problem can be solved by appeal to parallel universes – how can we deal with the other problems expressed by [1] and [2]? Two years ago, I thought that we should save the principle of contradiction, that is we should not allow that p & ~p, while at the same time *reject* the law of excluded middle. That is, I thought we should admit that some propositions are *neither true nor false*: ~($p \lor$

$\sim p$). We could then say that the cat is neither alive nor dead, instead of saying that she is alive as well as dead.

But this approach does not work. Because if we give up the law of excluded middle, then the principle of contradiction breaks down as well. This can also be proven by sentential logic.

(1) Assumption: $\sim(p \vee \sim p)$
(2) $\sim p \mathbin{\&} \sim\sim p$
(3) $\sim p \mathbin{\&} p$
(4) $p \mathbin{\&} \sim p$

If we say that some proposition is neither true nor false, this means that it is not the case that it is true and it is not the case that it is false (1 and 2 express the same). But according to mathematical logic, to say that it is not the case that it is true is just to say that it is false. And to say that it is not the case that it is false is just the same as to say that it is true: $\sim\sim p$ and p mean the same. And then, we conclude with the statement that the proposition is true as well as false (3 and 4); and this means, we come exactly to the statement that was the beginning of all the trouble above (the trouble with the moon that consists of ice cream).[7]

---

[7] How the law of excluded middle and the principle of contradiction are related to each other, became clear to me when I read Timothy Williamson (2007: 32).

1.4 The Alternative to Relativism

Should we reject every form of relativism and instead claim that every proposition whatsoever does have an absolute truth value? This is indeed what I find most plausible. It would be, as it were, the "comeback" of an old tradition that goes back perhaps to Plato, who thought that truth has a permanent existence, independently of our opinions.

> **The Comeback of Absolute Truth** =df. the thesis that every proposition has an absolute truth value.

But of course, propositions like [1], [2] and [3] are a problem, and this is, I think, one reason why many people find relativism appealing. Does the relativist have any chance? Of course, he can avoid the logical problem by rejecting logic itself. He could replace mathematical logic by some other, 'non-consistent' logic, or something similar. But it is far from clear how this could work. Mathematical logic is extremely successful, not only as a fundament of science but also in the field of argumentation. If we give up mathematical logic, then, I think, we will face even more difficult problems. And furthermore: You would have to explain why some propositions are indeed absolutely true – why no relativism is possible in these cases (such as the truth of the holocaust and the moral wrongness of extreme unfairness).[8]

---

[8] Motivated by quantum mechanical phenomena, Engesser et al. developed a new logical system that takes a step towards relativism. (2007) Unfortunately, so far I have not been able to understand the details of this approach.

My simple answer to the problems of relativism is that relativism is, I guess, false: Every proposition does have an absolute truth value. There are some cases where nobody, or nearly nobody, *knows which* truth value the proposition has. But from this it does not follow that any proposition does not *have* an absolute truth value. Look at this proposition:

[6] At November 21st, 1940, president Franklin Roosevelt was, for some seconds, thinking of bacon.

It may be that nobody knows whether this proposition is true. But of course, the proposition *is* either true or false. Either he thought of bacon at this time, or he did not. And this truth value is absolute: It does not change and not depend on the perspective. The same could be true of the propositions [1], [2] and [3], if these propositions make sense at all.

At the beginning of this chapter, I said that one reason why people become relativists may be that they do not like fundamentalism. One might think: "If you say that every proposition is either absolutely true or absolutely false, then you do not allow any discourse; you expect everybody to think what is right in your opinion. This is how religious fundamentalism works. This is how Stalin thought. This is unacceptable." But such a criticism is not adequate. To say that every proposition has an absolute truth value is not to say that there should not be a democratic discourse. Because to say that every proposition has an absolute truth value is not to say that anybody *knows* the truth value of any proposition. The problem with the communist one-party system was not that they thought there is only absolute truth; the problem was that they thought *that they know what's true*.

As soon as we remember the distinction between having an absolute truth-value and knowing the truth-value, we can reject relativism without any danger. Every proposition that has sense at all is, I think, either absolutely true or absolutely false. But nobody has the right to think that he or she knows, in every case, which propositions are absolutely true and which are absolutely false.

1.5 Additional Remarks

1) Knowledge is a much harder topic than truth. In this chapter, I argued for the thesis that every proposition, if it makes sense at all, is either absolutely true or absolutely false. This is quite simple, and the simplicity should not surprise anybody. Note, for example, that 'p' means the same as "'p' is true'; in logic, we would symbolize both in exactly the same way. This indicates that truth is something quite simple. But knowledge is not that simple: It is plausible to assume that if a proposition is known, then it is true; but the opposite is not true: Not every true proposition is known. Even if Paula's belief that p is true *and justified*, then it does not follow that Paula knows that p. This is what Edmund Gettier showed (1963). Imagine the following situation:

Paula wants to know the time. She looks at the clock in her parents' apartment – a clock that is usually very reliable. The clock shows '5 o'clock'. She forms the belief p that it is 5 o'clock. This belief is justified: Paula has no reason for significant distrust, because the clock is usually reliable. But it turns out that the clock *always* shows 5 o'clock; since the last day the clock does not work any more. However, Paula is lucky: It is indeed 5 o'clock! She looked at the clock at 5 o'clock. So what properties does Paula's belief *p* have, at the moment when she looks at the clock and thinks that it is 5 o'clock? The belief is, first, justified (she has good reason to believe that it is 5 o'clock, because she has good reason to trust the clock). The belief is, secondly, true. But Paula does not *know* that it is 5 o'clock. She perhaps thinks that she knows it, but she does not know it. The truth of her belief was just luck. I do not want to get deeper into theories of knowledge; the example may be enough to illustrate that knowledge is a complicated phenomenon, more complicated than truth.[9]

2) I should say something to a problem that seems to follow from certain paradoxes, such as Russell's famous paradox: Does the set that includes all and only those sets that do not include themselves include itself? This is, for our purposes, the same as the Barber paradox: Does the barber who shaves all and only those men that do not shave themselves shame himself? We should look at this problem step by step. This is the Barber (I write 'Barber' with a capital letter 'B' whenever I refer to this certain barber):

> [7] the barber who shaves all men, and only those men, that do not shave themselves.

---

[9] See also chapter 3 of this book, which discusses the relation between truth and knowledge.

Does the Barber shave himself? Suppose that the Barber [7] shaves himself. Then he is a man who does shave himself; therefore, according to the definition, he does not shave himself. (Because he does not shave any man that does shave himself; he only shaves men that do not shave themselves.) Suppose that the Barber does not shave himself. Then he is a man that does not shave himself; and according to the definition, he therefore shaves himself. (Because he shaves every man that does not shave himself.) In other words: If the sentence

[8] The Barber defined in [7] shaves himself.

is true, then it is false. And if [8] is false, then [8] is true. This looks like a proposition that is both true and false; and *this* looks like relativism.

One could try to solve the problem by not attributing any truth value to sentence [8]; one could say that [8] is a proposition that is neither true nor false. But of course, this would also lead to relativism. Does the anti-relativist, the absolute truth theorist, have any chance to explain the Barber case?

Yes: The sentence [8] is not a proposition at all. Because the name 'the Barber defined in [7]' does not refer to anything; there is no barber who shaves all men that do not shave themselves, and there could not possibly be one. Such a barber is impossible. *If* there were such a barber, then there would be a contradiction: The Barber would shave himself, and he would not shave himself. For those of us who have some basic knowledge of logic, I give this rough logical derivation that shows how the existence of the Barber would lead to a contradiction – and that, therefore, his existence is simply impossible.[10]

(1)	Assumption: The Barber defined in [7] exists.	p
(2)	If the Barber defined in [7] exists, then either he shaves himself, or he does not shave himself.	$p \rightarrow (q \vee \sim q)$
(3)	Therefore, either he shaves himself, or he does not shave himself. (1, 2, *modus ponens*)	$q \vee \sim q$
(4)	First case: He shaves himself.	q
(5)	If he shaves himself, then he does not shave himself.	$q \rightarrow \sim q$
(6)	Therefore, he does not shave himself. (4, 5, *modus ponens*)	$\sim q$
(7)	Therefore, contradiction. (on 4 and 6)	X
(8)	Second case: He does not shave himself.	$\sim q$
(9)	If he does not shave himself, then he shaves himself.	$\sim q \rightarrow q$
(10)	Therefore, he shaves himself. (8, 9, *modus ponens*)	q
(11)	Therefore, contradiction. (on 8 and 10)	X

---

[10] The right column expresses the argument with logical symbols. 'p' means 'The Barber defined in [7] exists' and 'q' means 'The Barber shaves himself'.

(12)	Therefore, the assumption that the barber exists is false. (*reductio ad absurdum*)	~p

This is a formally valid argument, although it could be presented in more detail (for example by using predicate logic). Since it is a logical derivation, the conclusion is – if the premises are true – *necessarily* true. This means that necessarily, there is no such barber as defined in [7]. The trouble never occurs; it is not possible that the term [7] refers to anything, and sentence [8] is not a (significant) proposition. To say that the barber who shaves all and only the men that do not shave themselves shaves himself, or to say that he does *not* shave himself, is without sense; it makes as little sense as to claim that the yellow elephant in my room shaves himself, or that he does not shave himself. (The elephant claim is even more plausible than the Barber case! Because it is at least logically possible that there is such an elephant.)

3) Now I finished the discussion of relativism and should say which theory of truth I support. Rather than giving any complete account, and rather than evaluating every or many existing theories of truth, I will only note some thoughts that are in line with the spirit of this chapter. I wrote above that truth is a rather simple topic, because "*p*' is true' simply means the same as '*p*'. This may be called a minimalist theory of truth, or a redundancy theory of truth.

> **Minimalist account** =df. **redundancy account** =df. the thesis that "*p*' is true' simply means the same as '*p*'.

According to this position, to say that a certain proposition is true does not add anything significant; it is merely redundant. Instead of saying "The proposition 'Laura's car is blue' is true", I could simply assert "Laura's car is blue". Both means the same.[11] But if this minimalist account of truth is correct, then why do we need the word 'true' at all? If "p' is true' means the same as 'p', then why not save time and always choose the second option: skip the truth? Do we speak about truth only because "p' is true' has a slightly different connotation than 'p'?

I think there is another reason why we use words such as 'true'. And this reason is compatible with the minimalist or redundancy approach. Imagine that Pete told me that Sarah is an idiot and not very trustworthy, and now I decided to agree with him. I want to express what Pete said and that I agree with him. I could say:

> [9] Pete said "Sarah is an idiot and not very trustworthy", and (indeed), Sarah is an idiot and not very trustworthy.

But this is a rather long sentence, and it does not sound very well. I would better say:

---

[11] However, it should be noted that in every-day life, to say "p" involves a slightly different connotation than saying "p is true". If I say "It is true that Laura's car is blue", or "The proposition 'Laura's car is blue' is true", then I emphasize that I am pretty sure about the color of Laura's car. If I only say "Laura's car is blue", then there is perhaps no such connotation; it may be that I *guess* that her car is blue, but that I am not quite sure about this.

[10] Pete said "Sarah is an idiot and not very trustworthy", and this is true.

The sentences [9] and [10] express the same, but [10] is shorter and simpler than [9]. So the use of the word 'true' has not added any new information, but it is pragmatically helpful. (Of course, there are similar ways to express the same. I could say "Pete said … and he is *right*." Or "Pete said … and I *agree* with him.")

Is there anything more to say about truth? (Or in more adequate words: Is there more to say about 'being true'? Because the noun 'truth' may be misleading. There is no thing that the term 'truth' refers to; there is no 'the Truth', as there are the United States of America or the Statue of Liberty. Whenever I say 'truth', I simply refer to the notion of 'being true'.) If "p' is true' can be reduced to 'p', and we need truth only to simplify some of our sentences, then, can there be any significant theory of truth?

If there can be any more significant theory of truth, then it is a realistic theory. A realistic theory of truth claims that the truth or falsity (the truth-value) of a proposition depends on the world. Whether the proposition 'There are many poor people around the world' is true, depends on the actual poverty that is there. (The world makes this proposition true.[12]) This should be self-evident; and I mention it only because it

---

[12] This does not mean that human beings are not responsible for poverty. They are, in many cases. To say that the world makes the proposition true and to say that human beings make the proposition true, is no contradiction. Human beings are parts of the world.

seems that this realistic program is controversial. For example, I heard of a coherence theory of truth, which states (roughly) that a proposition is true if and only if it is coherent. But this requirement is, to mention only one point, not sufficient. It may be that somebody has completely coherent opinions; they are all consistent with each other, and none of the opinions is self-contradictory etc. But still, it may be that all of these opinions are false. It may be that this person lives (mentally) in a fantasy-world that has not much to do with the real world. In this case, it would be implausible to regard his opinions as true. Coherence does not guarantee truth. Truth-values depend on the world.

Can a realistic theory of truth be developed in more detail? Frank Hofmann thinks that this is possible, and at the same time he does not give up the minimalist approach. (2008)

> "Something [p] is true if and only if the world behaves as it [p] says that it behaves. (Or: if the things are as they are represented by the thing that has the truth-value.) This 'as' or 'to be as' contains, so to speak, the whole idea of truth – and in those expressions there is also the whole difficulty. If we want to understand truth better, then it is necessary to analyze this 'to be as'. And with this we should start now." (15; my translation)

If I understand these matters correctly, then the idea is something like this: We want to understand truth. "p' is true' means 'p'. But what makes it the case that p? It is the case that p if and only if the world is as p asserts that the world is. (If p is the proposition that the world contains seven billion human beings, then p is the case if and only if the world contains seven billion human beings.) This should, Hofmann thinks, be analyzed in more detail. How exactly does the world have to be to make a certain proposition true or false? What exactly is the relation between the world and the proposition? Hofmann thinks that a correspondence theory of truth can help us here (this becomes already clear in the quotation above, where he emphasizes on the expression 'to be as'), and he spells out this correspondence theory in terms of truth-makers. (cf. 19 et seq.) I do not have any argument against correspondence theories. But I question whether they can provide a better understanding of truth than the minimalist theory already did.

What is the main idea of correspondence and truth-maker theories of truth? For a proposition to be true, there has to be a correspondence between the proposition and the world. I regard this as obviously true. If a proposition asserts that Lisa has blond hair, then this proposition is true if and only if there is (in the world) blond hair on Lisa's head. (I let problems that are related to the objectivity or subjectivity of colors aside.) If the proposition speaks of Lisa's blond hair, and there is such blond hair on her head, then this can be called a correspondence between the proposition and the world. One could also say that the blond hair on Lisa's head is the truth-maker of the proposition that Lisa has blond hair. Or one could say that the *fact* that Lisa has blond hair is the truth-maker of the proposition. (Hofmann would prefer the second claim.) This could be generalized to such a theory of truth:

Correspondence and truth-maker theory of truth =df. '*p*' is true if and only if there is some *x* in the world such that if there is *x*, then *p*.

This, of course, is a simplification, and Hofmann adds many details.[13] But let us discuss the general structure of truth-maker and correspondence theories – and the question whether they provide an understanding of truth that goes beyond the simple principle that the minimalist account gave us (that "*p* is true' means the same as '*p*').

Note that correspondence and truth-maker theories do not say much more than "'*p*' is true if and only if … *p*". The structure is the same as the structure of the minimalist account. Hofmann admits this; he admits that there is some kind of circularity in the principle (he calls it "implicitly circular"), and that you already have to possess an understanding of truth to understand the theory of truth. The theory does not provide such an understanding to somebody that does not already have some understanding of truth.

"… Somebody who did not possess any understanding of truth, could not reach the understanding of truth through

---

[13] Cf. Hofmann (2008: especially 34 et seq.). That the correspondence and truth-maker approach that I sketched is too simple, becomes obvious in cases such as 'Santa Clause does not exist'. This proposition is true, but there is no truth maker (there could not possibly be any truth-maker, because the proposition asserts that *there is no* Santa Clause). Those negative propositions need a special discussion. Furthermore, there are problems with necessary propositions, which Hofmann wants to solve with his own truth-maker approach.

such a definition alone. Without having at least an implicit understanding of truth, as it is required for the understanding of propositions and representation, one could not reach an understanding of truth with the implicitly circular definition." (29; my translation)

Every theory of truth that I heard of is either false or in this sense circular. I doubt whether we can say much about truth. Of course, we can discuss some questions that are related to truth; such as the plausibility or implausibility of relativism, which was the main topic of this chapter, or some details concerning truth-makers. But truth *itself* does not seem to say much more than "p' is true if and only if p'. And whether p is the case or not, this is 'decided' by the world.

2 On the Relation between Philosophy and Logic

2.1 Introduction

In this book, logic plays an essential role: I use logic at many points to argue for my theses that are related to truth and knowledge. But is it legitimate to use logic in philosophy? And if it is: *How* should logic be used? What is the relation between philosophy and logic?

Nobody can honestly deny that philosophy and logic are closely related. I will not give a definition of the terms 'philosophy' and 'logic'; this attempt would not be successful. I assume that we all have a relatively common – and relatively adequate – rough idea of what 'philosophy' is and what 'logic' is. In philosophy, usually only *arguments* are relevant. Logic is concerned with the question what follows from what (with necessity). It is concerned with the question which arguments are valid and which not. So what we have here are two disciplines, one of which focuses on concrete arguments (philosophy) and the other one proves which arguments are valid (logic). This suggests that philosophy and logic are indeed closely related: Philosophy needs logic.

It seems that based on this observation, some people came to believe that philosophy is identical to logic; or that philosophy is reducible, should be reduced, to logic. I regard these positions as unbelievable mistakes. To think that philosophy should or could merely consist of logical thought, is a new scandal of philosophy, namely a scandal of some parts of analytic philosophy. In this chapter, I will argue for the thesis that – although the relation between philosophy and logic is close – philosophy is not reducible to logic. Philosophy needs logic, but philosophy also needs much more.

I will not invest much time in the question *who* said or implicitly thought that philosophy is merely a logical enterprise. Most philosophers of the current time would not say that they believe in the reducibility of philosophy to logic; but however, when it comes to their actual philosophical work, some of them do completely or mainly focus on logic, and regard everything that comes from fields other than logic as irrelevant for the philosophical discourse. One of the origins of the belief that philosophy should be restricted to logical considerations, may be Bertrand Russell, who said, as far as I remember, that every philosophical problem is a logical problem. (He said that either it is not really a philosophical problem, or it is a logical problem.)

Surely, it is possible to define 'logic' in a very broad way – so broad that logic includes every discipline that deals with arguments. In this case, it is possible, but also trivial, that philosophy is reducible to logic. But the point is that people who seem to think that philosophy is reducible to logic, do not use such a broad definition of logic. They think of logic as merely *formal* logic. They believe or suggest that philosophy could and should be identical to formal logic, or that philosophy could and should be reduced to formal logic. That is the problematic – and false – position. (In this chapter, whenever I say 'logic', I refer to formal logic.)

What is (formal) logic? I already said that the attempt to give precise definitions would be unsuccessful. But it should at least be noted that when I write 'logic', I do not refer to what Kant meant when he used the term 'logic' in his *Kritik der reinen Vernunft* (*Critique of Pure Reason*). The main part of his book is entitled 'Transcendental Logic'. But his book does not seem to have a close relation to formal logic; instead, it consists of more or less rigid, more or less convincing arguments. In his opinion, this is enough to call the discovery 'logic'. But of course, this was another time, and we use the term 'logic' differently. Here, 'logic' means formal logic only. According to that rough definition, this here is a typical piece of logic:

(1) $p \rightarrow q$
(2) p
(3) Therefore, q.

Proposition (3) follows from the premises (1) and (2) by *modus ponens*. This here is another example of (formal!) logic:

(1) Susie recommends Paul's favorite book to Hannah's daughter.
(2) Paul's favorite book is identical to Mortimer Adler's third book.
(3) Therefore, Susie recommends Mortimer Adler's third book to Hannah's daughter.

Proposition (3) follows from (1) and (2) by Leibniz's law, a rule in identity logic. But is this argument a piece of (formal) logic? Yes. It seems that the argument consists of sentences, and not of formal symbols. But nevertheless, the argument is indeed identical to an argument in formal logic – if we give an adequate lexicon. For those who are interested in logic, I will explain this with some words. This is a possible lexicon:

s	:	Susie
$R\,[\alpha, \beta, \gamma]$	:	α recommends β to γ
p	:	Paul
$f(\alpha)$	:	α's favorite book
h	:	Hannah
$d(\alpha)$	:	α's daughter
m	:	Mortimer Adler
$t(\alpha)$	:	α's third book

Then, the argument can be stated as follows:

(1) $R\,[\,s, f(p), d(h)\,]$
(2) $f(p) = t(m)$
(3) Therefore, $R\,[\,s, t(m), d(h)\,]$

This is the same argument as the written one above. Whether an argument is presented in symbols or in natural language is irrelevant for the question whether the argument is a piece of (formal) logic or not. What makes an argument a (valid) argument in formal logic is simply the fact that the conclusion follows necessarily from the premises, by the laws of logic. Symbols usually provide the clearest form of presentation; but logic can operate with natural language, as well.

Now it should be clear enough what 'logic' means; and it should be clear enough what position I want to reject. But what is my argument? Why is philosophy not reducible to logic? Because philosophy tries to give us true philosophical statements. And logic alone cannot give us true philosophical statements. It is especially the last claim – that logic alone cannot give us true philosophical statements – that I will argue for. But the first claim – that philosophy ties to provide true statements – may also be questioned.

I heard people saying that philosophy does not search for truth, or that philosophy does not search for answers; that philosophy only tries to provide interesting *questions*. People who say that may have a point, but their position is nevertheless confused. I will not discuss in detail what the problems of this position are; this would be material for another chapter. But one thing should be noted: If philosophy were not concerned with true statements, then no academic discourse would be possible in philosophy. Everybody could present something, and nobody could criticize the other one, because nobody would insist on the truth of the very things that she says. The first one would say "Is *a* true?", the second one would say "Is *b* true?", and the third one would say "Is *c* true?". And there is no basis for discourse, because nobody is interested in making a statement. This is a ridiculous – and fortunately false – picture. Let us stop here and assume that philosophy tries to provide true philosophical statements. I said above that logic alone cannot provide true philosophical statements. This is why:

2.2 Logically Valid, but False

Logic does not have much to do with truth. There are infinitely many logically valid derivations, or arguments, that have a false conclusion. This here is an example:

(1) The human mind is timeless. (premise)
(2) Everything that is timeless survives forever. (premise)
(3) Therefore, the human mind survives forever.

It seems that Plato believed something like this (although, if he had spoken English, he would probably have preferred the term 'human soul'). The argument is formally valid; it could be formalized this way:

(1) $\forall x\,(Mx \rightarrow Tx)$
(2) $\forall x\,(Tx \rightarrow Sx)$
(3) Therefore, $\forall x\,(Mx \rightarrow Sx)$
    (follows by predicate logic)

But nevertheless, what the argument finally states – that the human mind survives forever – is false, or at least: Much more would have to be done to make it plausible that the human mind survives forever. The above argument, although logically valid, does not give us any reason to think that the human mind survives forever. This is especially because of the first premise: The argument depends on the problematic claim that the human mind is timeless. There is, I assume, much more evidence for the opposite claim, this is the claim that the human mind exists in space and time. But however, it would lead us astray if we talked about the deep philosophical problems here. Let us summarize that logic does not *give* us philosophical truth. If you look at an argument from a merely logical point of view, then you can only say "The argument is valid" or "The argument is not valid". In the case above, the argument is valid. This means nothing more than: Necessarily, if the premises that you gave me are true, then the conclusion that you gave me is true. But *are* the premises true? Is the proposition $\forall x\,(\,Mx \to Tx\,)$ true? This is something that logic alone cannot give us. Logic alone does not tell us whether the human mind is timeless. We have to look out of the window, we have to go and to consider science and to think clearly about evidence; logic alone is not the key.

2.3 Logically Invalid, but True

It is not only that logic is not sufficient for philosophical truth; logic is not necessary for philosophical truth, either. This argument is logically invalid:

(1) Human beings are completely material.
(2) Everything that is completely material is subject to the laws of nature.
(3) Therefore, human beings do not have a free will.

The invalidity can be seen easier when the argument is formalized:

(1) $\forall x\,(\,Hx \to Cx\,)$
(2) $\forall x\,(\,Cx \to Lx\,)$
(3) Therefore, $\forall x\,(\,Hx \to {\sim} Fx\,)$

The conclusion does not follow from the premises. (Note that the conclusion contains the predicate F, which does not even occur in the premises.) But although the argument is logically invalid, the conclusion is, I think, a true philosophical thesis: the thesis that human beings do not have a free will.[14] So philosophical truth does not require logical validity. Of course, the truth of the thesis that human beings do not have free will is controversial; if you do not like the example, then I can give you this uncontroversial one (which is less interesting and presumably not philosophical):

(1) Every human being is an animal.
(2) Every human being is a fish.
(3) Therefore, every fish is an animal.

Here we clearly have a true conclusion. But the argument is not valid: The conclusion does not follow from the premises. Logical validity is not necessary for truth.

I already said that logic does not have so much to do with truth. It seems that the only connection between logic and truth consists in the fact that if an argument is logically valid, then necessarily, *if* the premises are true, then the conclusion is true. This of course allows for the option that a logically invalid argument has a true conclusion, even an interesting philosophical truth; and it allows for the option that a logically valid argument has a false or even philosophically ridiculous conclusion. This is, therefore, why philosophy cannot be reduced to logic: Even if your argument does not satisfy the requirements made by logic, it can nevertheless

---

[14] See also chapter 7 of this book.

have a philosophically true conclusion; and on the other hand, even if you satisfy all the logical requirements, it may be that your philosophical conclusion is false (namely, in the case that one of your premises is false).

2.4 Truths Given by Logic Alone

I should add one more detail. It is not exactly true that the only connection between logic and truth is the fact that a logically valid argument guarantees the truth-conduciveness from the premises to the conclusion. Logic can also assert truths that do not depend on any premises. These are necessary truths, namely logical or mathematical truths. This here is an example:

$$(\sim a \,\&\, \sim b) \rightarrow \sim a$$

This is indeed a true proposition which is produced by logic alone (and whose truth can be shown by sentential logic in one step). Let 'a' mean 'The world is perfectly good', and let 'b' mean 'The world is completely bad'. Then the above proposition asserts this: 'If it is not the case that the world is perfectly good and not the case that the world is completely bad, then it is not the case that the world is perfectly good'. This is necessarily true; but it is not of much philosophical interest.

The truths that logic can offer by itself, are only necessary truths, and these are of much interest for mathematicians and logicians, but not for most other fields in philosophy.

Philosophy is usually interested in philosophical truths, not in necessary or mathematical truths.

2.5 Conclusions

Let me summarize the three most important points:

- In the case of arguments, logic does not guarantee truth.
- Furthermore, logical validity is not even necessary for truth.
- And the truths that logic can offer by itself are mathematical truths, and therefore normally not of much philosophical interest.

It seems to me that the first of these points is the crucial one. Let us remember the argument for the presumably false philosophical thesis that the human mind survives forever. (Some people may think that this is not a false *philosophical* thesis, but a false *scientific* thesis. Then you can just use another example, one that is more clearly philosophical.) The argument for the thesis that the human mind survives forever was logically valid. Logic can prove that all the requirements made by logic are satisfied. (To do this, you need the logical rules Universal-Out and *modus ponens*.) So you can prove the logical validity. But the conclusion is nevertheless false! This is possible because the argument contains a false premise. But logic alone does not give you that one of the premises is false. You could try to find another logically valid argument that shows that one the premises of our argument was false. But the truth of the conclusion of this new argument would, again, depend on the truth of the premises of this new argument. Everything that logic can offer to philosophy is a relation between premises and a conclusion. But if you do not know whether the premises are true, then you do not know whether the conclusion is true – no matter how good you are in logic.

2.6 Additional Remarks

If logic cannot give me the truth of the premises: *What* can give me the truth of the premises? In other words: What does philosophy need, if logic is not enough? This is a deep question, too deep for this chapter. I only promised to show that philosophy is not reducible (and of course not identical) to logic; I would never promise that I could say what the alternatives are. Some hints should be enough. I think that philosophical premises can come from *anywhere*.

Sometimes philosophy can get true premises from natural sciences. For example, some people may regard it as a true thesis in physics that determinism is false. Then, you could use the thesis that determinism is false as a premise in a philosophical argument. Together with other premises, you could build up a logically valid argument with the conclusion that nobody could ever predict the behavior of a human being with certainty. This is a philosophically relevant – and probably true – thesis. What philosophy is doing here is this: getting theses from natural sciences, putting them together with other premises (perhaps also from natural sciences), combining them to a logically valid argument, and reaching a philosophical conclusion.

In other cases, philosophy can get true premises from social sciences. Very often, the premises are neither from natural science nor from social science, but from philosophy itself. In a text written by the medieval philosopher Thomas Aquinas, I found this argument for the existence of God: (Thomas 2010)[15]

> "Everything that is moved is moved by another. That some things are in motion – for example, the sun – is evident from sense. Therefore, it is moved by something else that moves it. This mover is itself either moved or not moved. If it is not, we have reached our conclusion – namely, that we must posit some unmoved mover. This we call God. If it is moved, it is moved by another mover. We must, consequently, either proceed to infinity, or we must arrive at some unmoved mover. Now, it is not possible to proceed to infinity. Hence, we must posit some prime unmoved mover." (184)

It is possible to interpret this argument in a way that allows for a logically valid presentation; I tried this, and it turned out to be a very long argument (20 lines). So let us better focus on the interesting points. Thomas' conclusion is essentially this: There is a mover who is himself not moved (an unmoved mover, or God). The most important premises are these: Some things that we see are moved; everything that is moved is moved by something else; the chain of

---

[15] It should be noted that according to Thomas, the definition of 'God' seems to be 'unmoved mover'. If somebody does not share this definition – I, for example, do not share it – then he will not regard Thomas' argument as an argument for the existence of God. See also chapter 7 of this book.

movers (*a* moves *b* moves *c* …) cannot proceed to infinity; if the chain cannot proceed to infinity, then there is a mover who is himself not moved (God).

Is one of the premises false? Logic cannot provide us an answer. For example, the premise that everything that is moved is moved by something else, is problematic. Could it not be that some things move themselves? Could it not be that some things, or even all things, are moved by forces that are not themselves *things*? These are deep philosophical questions, which are obviously related to physics. It does not seem that logic alone gives the answer, or that the answer is reducible to logic.

Another crucial premise is this: To avoid an *infinite regress*, Thomas thinks, we have to posit an unmoved mover. But why should it not be like a circle? Morgan moves Kathleen, Kathleen moves Angie, Angie moves Morgan. If the world works like this picture – although in a much more complicated manner –, then it seems that the infinite regress could be avoided without proposing something that moves and is itself unmoved. But to decide whether this is plausible is not a logical enterprise: One has to go outside and to see how the world works, and the best method would perhaps be a philosophical interpretation of natural science. Aquinas' argument for the existence of God is an example of an argument whose premises themselves depend on other philosophical theories. Natural science, social science and philosophy can provide premises that can be used for philosophical arguments. It's not logic alone.

Whether we regard a philosophical premise as true, can also depend on our *intuitions*. What is knowledge? In chapter 1, I mentioned an argument against the thesis that knowledge is justified true belief. The crucial premise of such an argument is this: There are possible cases where we have a justified true belief that *p*, but nevertheless we do not know that *p*. Whether this premise is true, depends on our interpretation of certain thought experiments; and our interpretation depends on our intuitions. In the previous chapter, I used this example: Paula looks at the clock, the clock says '5 o'clock'. She is justified in trusting the clock, so she is justified in believing that it is 5 o'clock. Indeed this belief is true. But – what Paula does not know – the clock always shows 5 o'clock, it does not work any more. Paula was lucky that she looked at the clock just in the moment when it was indeed 5 o'clock. Does her belief that it is 5 o'clock count as knowledge, in this case? There is widespread agreement that the answer is 'No'. But somebody could have another intuition and claim: "Yes, Paula has knowledge. She was lucky, but she nevertheless knew that it is 5 o'clock! If a belief is true and justified: This is enough for its being knowledge! Knowledge is justified true belief." Somebody could judge in the same way in all the Gettier-style thought experiments. It would be odd – but there is no logical proof against such an odd intuition. So philosophical arguments can essentially depend on our intuitions. Sometimes everybody or nearly everybody has the same intuition, and sometimes not.

Is lying always morally wrong? It seems that the bible says this: in the second book of Moses, Exodus 20:16. But my teacher Fred Feldman, for example, gave this thought experiment (which is indeed more than a thought experiment: it is a historical fact). Nazis come to somebody's house (call the owner of the house 'Müller') and ask this question: "Is there a Jew in your house?". Suppose that Müller indeed hides a Jewish friend in his house, to save the Jew from the Nazis. And suppose that if Müller lies to the Nazis, then the probability that the Jew is not found is higher than in case that Müller does not lie to the Nazis. Is it, in this case, morally wrong to lie? Most people, including me, would say No. This can be used as a premise in an argument with the conclusion that it is not always morally wrong to lie. But if somebody has other intuitions, then the premise is not true. Somebody might have the intuition that even in Müller's case, it is morally wrong to lie. (This sounds very odd, and I think it is unacceptable. But perhaps somebody thinks that it is always morally wrong to lie, even in Müller's case, and that it would *also* be morally wrong not to lie – because this could kill the Jew. So Müller should decide which of the morally wrong acts is worse. Presumably, it would turn out that not to lie is worse than to lie.)

How important are intuitions for philosophy? If all philosophical arguments eventually depend on intuitions, then philosophy can never discover anything that we do not already believe. Philosophy could never find out whether our intuitions are right, because philosophical arguments would presuppose that our intuitions are right. Such a view has indeed been argued for, namely by the popular philosopher Mortimer J. Adler (1985). He speaks of "common-sense knowledge", which means essentially the same as what I call "intuition".

> "Theoretical philosophy is an analytical and reflective refinement of what we know by common sense in the light of common experience. Our common-sense knowledge is deepened, illuminated, and elaborated by philosophical thought. There is little if any sound philosophy that conflicts with our common-sense knowledge, for both are based on the common human experience out of which they emerge." (106)

I think that such a view overestimates the importance of intuitions for philosophy. Surely, our intuitions (or our common-sense knowledge) very often or always play a role in philosophical thinking, especially in the interpretation of thought experiments. But intuitions do not always do the job *alone*. (Furthermore, it is not even clear what Adler means when he says that our common-sense knowledge is "deepened" by philosophy.) Above, I already mentioned the importance of science for philosophy. If science does not depend on intuitions alone, then philosophy does not depend on intuitions alone.

If the truth of philosophical statements depends on natural science, social science, and philosophy itself, including intuitions: Then what can logic do for philosophy? Suppose there is an argument in philosophy, and all of the premises are true. (I indeed think that every premise is either true or false – although we often do not *know* whether they are true or false, since we have different intuitions etc.) If the argument is *not* logically valid, then, even if all premises are true, it is possible that the conclusion is false. So somebody, for example Marc, could say: "I do not claim that any of your premises is false. But I nevertheless do not agree with your philosophical statement in the conclusion." Marc would therefore argue against the statement without saying for what exact reason he disagrees. In a philosophical discourse, this is sad. I want to know for what reason Marc does not accept my conclusion. So I better present my argument in a logically valid way. Then, necessarily, if all the premises are true, then my conclusion is true. So if Marc thinks that the conclusion is false, then he *must* think that there is a false premise. (Otherwise, he would be irrational to an unbelievable extent.) So in the discourse, I can force him: "Marc, you say that you disagree with the conclusion. So show me which of the premises should be regarded as false!" *So philosophy needs logic especially for the purposes of presentation and discourse.*

For example, a very short summary of the chapter is this:

(1)	If philosophy could be reduced to logic, then the truth of every philosophy statement would depend on logical validity only.	$p \rightarrow q$
(2)	It is not the case that the truth of every philosophical statement depends on logical validity only.	$\sim q$
(3)	Therefore, it is not the case that philosophy can be reduced to logic. (1, 2, *modus tollens*)	$\sim p$

This is a valid argument. So if the conclusion is false, then one of the premises is false. If you do not agree with my conclusion: Which of the premises is false? (The first premise should be regarded as unproblematic. The second is more difficult, but this is why I needed the whole chapter to argue for its truth.)

3 On the Relation between Truth and Knowledge

3.1 Introduction

In chapter 1, it became clear that probably every proposition is either true or false. But very often, we don't know whether a proposition is true or false. How often? What *do* we know? Do I know that the United States currently contain fifty states? Do I know that death is bad? That 2 + 3 is 5? That there is a God? That there is no God? That pure water is H_2O? That running is healthy? That my sister is happy? That she is my sister? Rather than answering those questions seperately, I will sketch some *general* conditions for knowledge. With the help of those general requirements, it may be easier to answer the questions about the status of particular beliefs. (But the evaluation of particular beliefs will remain a difficult business, even if a general understanding of knowledge is achieved.) My short discovery will mainly focus on the relation between knowledge and truth.

We discover the nature of knowledge – what does this mean? It seems that 'knowledge' is a word and that words can be defined in every way, arbitrarily (just as symbols can be defined arbitrarily). If this is the case, then, it seems, there is no general, true nature of knowledge. Everybody could define 'knowledge' however she wants, and the only thing that I could do is to add a further definition, which could perhaps be helpful for the book, but not more. And indeed, knowledge *is* a word, and everybody is free to define it however she wants; but this is not my goal here. What I am concerned with is the nature of knowledge, and the nature of knowledge, I assume, is the nature of the phenomenon that we usually talk about when we use the word 'knowledge'. I am concerned with the exact meaning of the word 'knowledge', how it is usually used.[16] It would not be useful to give a definition of 'knowledge' that is not connected to the usual use of the word.

One could question whether it is possible to discover any usual meaning of 'knowledge'. I admit, of course, that not everybody uses the word in exactly the same way. But it is obvious that there is some close relation between the ways how we use a particular word, such as the word 'knowledge'. There must be some common ground on which the uses of the word are based. If this were not the case – if, for example, everybody had something radically different in mind while using the word 'knowledge' –, then we would not understand each other and would not be able to discuss academic questions that are related to knowledge. But we do understand each other to some extent, and we do discuss questions that concern knowledge. So it can be assumed that a (more or less exact) common meaning of 'knowledge' exists. And I am here taking some steps to discover the nature of this common meaning.

---

[16] The word 'knowledge' is used in every-day life as well as in academic contexts; I am concerned with both, and I do not see any significant difference between the ordinary and the academic use of the word.

Is an analysis of the common use of a word useful? If we already understand each other, as I assumed, then why do we need any such analysis? We understand each other because we have some (mainly) *implicit* concept of knowledge in our mind. It may also be called an unconscious concept. We are able to talk about knowledge, but the concept is normally not made explicit. One goal of this short paper is to bring our common understanding of knowledge from the dark to the light. And the effect will be that we understand knowledge better.

This process is not unusual; compare, for example, the phenomenon lying. We somehow understand the verb 'to lie', and except for borderline cases, our implicit concept of lying is commonly shared. But this concept is normally not made explicit and needs some analysis, similar to the case of knowledge (although there are differences). When I asked people what 'to lie' means, then it was sometimes answered 'to say something that is not true'. But a slightly deeper analysis shows that this is not what we have in mind: If Paula says that Jeff is her father, because the does not know that he is indeed not her father, but her stepfather, then we would not say that Paula lies. Lying is a more complicated phenomenon. Even if we know that what we say is false, it may be that it is not a lie. (Compare the chapter on lying in Weidtmann/Evers, eds., 2009: especially p. 82.) Those examples show that we sometimes do not know *how* exactly we use the words that we use and implicitly understand. This paper tries to bring some clarity into the concept of 'knowledge'.

3.2 Knowledge and Beliefs

Whoever knows something, believes something. Or more exact: Everything that is known is a belief. This should be uncontroversial. Some people say "I do not believe, but I know that ...", which suggests that knowledge is distinct from beliefs; but this should be interpreted as a rhetorical move without much significance. Sometimes, the word 'belief' is understood quite narrowly, such that only doubtful beliefs are called 'beliefs'. Then, when I want to emphasize that I have no doubts, I say that "I do not believe, but I know". But I presuppose that 'belief' can be understood in a wider way. Knowledge is, as it were, a subgroup of beliefs. There are some beliefs that do not count as knowledge (such as Paula's false belief that the man who is sitting next to her is her biological father); and there other beliefs that count as knowledge (such as Paula's belief that Goethe was born in 1749, while we presuppose that Goethe was indeed born in 1749).

Is there another necessary condition for knowledge, in addition to the reasonable principle that only beliefs count as knowledge? Yes: truth.

3.3 Knowledge and Truth

Truth is a necessary condition for knowledge. It is impossible that: p is false *and* somebody knows that p. Again, there are exceptional cases where we use the word 'knowledge' as if truth were not necessary. For example, when somebody says: "I simply *knew* that he would marry Martha. But then he married Jennifer instead." But this is, as I said, exceptional, and it should be regarded as a rhetoric move. The belief that he would marry Martha was a false belief and not knowledge. It may be that the speaker had strong evidence for his marrying Martha (and this is why she says "I simply *knew* …"), but still, it was not knowledge. The beliefs that we call 'knowledge' are usually only true beliefs.

We can summarize the two results this way: to be a belief and to be true are two necessary conditions for knowledge. In other words: If p is known by subject x, then p is a belief of x and p is true. Using $K[\alpha, \beta]$ as a symbol for the predicate 'α knows β', $B[\alpha, \beta]$ for 'α believes β' and α for 'α is true', we can state:

[1] $Kxp \rightarrow (Bxp \,\&\, p)$[17]

This is the same as to say: If p is not a belief or not true, then p is not known.

[2] $(\sim\!Bxp \vee \sim\!p) \rightarrow \sim\!Kxp$

One might think that if truth is necessary for knowledge, then we cannot know anything, or at least not much. We should look at this idea closer. Most of us think that they know that water is H_2O. Our analysis has the consequence that our belief about water can only count as knowledge if this belief is true. But how can we be sure that the belief is true? I do not have the material or the ability to *prove* that

---

[17] Of course, this is a simplification. If exactness were more important than simplicity here, then we should use universals ($\forall$) for x and p.

water is H_2O; and most of us don't. Scientists have the required instruments, but even they sometimes go wrong with scientific theories. How can I be sure that water is indeed H_2O? If I am not completely sure that water is H_2O, then, it seems, it would be naïve simply to presuppose that the belief is true. And then, the belief cannot count as knowledge.

Or look at my belief that the United States contain fifty states. If a had a teacher that asked me "Do you know how many states the United States contain?", then I would probably say "Yes." But does my belief count as knowledge? Of course, I heard several times that the United States contain fifty states. But I have not seen them all. Surely, it would be odd to distrust all the sources where I heard or read that the number is fifty; but perhaps my memory goes wrong? Perhaps you would say that my memory is not so bad. But I remember cases where I was pretty sure about something and then it turned out that I was wrong, perhaps because of a false memory. Why should this not be the case here?

There were cases where men disguised themselves as women to win the Olympic games in the women's championship. Now imagine that during the women's competition and directly after it, no athlete had the idea that the fastest sprinter in this competition is indeed a man. And imagine an interview with the woman that came second. She believed that she is the second fastest woman. If she had been asked whether she *knows* that she is the second fastest woman, she would have answered "Yes". (Perhaps this would have been so obvious to her that the question seemed strange.) But however, the belief was false. She was the fastest woman, because the person who came first was a man.

Comparable surprises can always happen, it seems; what we regard as true may be false; and therefore, it seems, we cannot know anything, or at least not much. Some would even say that the whole sense experience that we have got does never constitute knowledge. This is perhaps what Descartes had in mind when he wrote the *Meditationes*, and what Socrates had in mind when he said that he knows that he does not know.

What I would like to argue for is that such a skeptical consequence is exaggerated. The principle that truth is necessary for knowledge, does not have the consequence that we do not know anything, and it does not even have the consequence that we do not know much. Of course, for all I know, it is *possible* that the United States do not contain fifty states. (This is both epistemically possible – I am not completely sure that the United States contain fifty states – as well as metaphysically possible.) It is possible that the belief that the U. S. contain fifty states is false. And then, in this possible case, my belief does not count as knowledge. But *in case* that the U. S. do indeed contain fifty states, then my belief counts as knowledge.

It is true that p is known only if p is true; but this does not mean that p is true only if p is *necessarily* true. Necessary truth is not a requirement. According to my former academic teacher Wolfgang Spohn, this is the origin of the confusion. The principle that truth is necessary for knowledge, which can roughly be symbolized by

[3] $Kp \rightarrow p$,

is a necessarily true principle. It is necessary because it follows from the meaning of the word 'knowledge'. So we can add the 'necessary' symbol $\square$ and write:

[4] $\square(Kp \rightarrow p)$

But to say that the *principle* is necessary true is not to say that p is necessarily true. To say that p is necessarily true would mean this:

[5] $Kp \rightarrow \square p$

And this is false. It is not a consequence of any of the discussed principles [1], [2], [3] and [4]. The two different statements [4] and [5] should not be confused. If [5] were true, then we could only know necessary truths, for example mathematical truths. But I do not see any argument for this claim. The belief p counts as knowledge only if p is true; the question whether p is a necessary or a contingent truth is another question. If it turned out that $2 + 3 \neq 5$, then just in this moment it has also turned out that our belief that $2 + 3 = 5$ does not constitute knowledge (and that it has never constituted knowledge). But *if* it is true that $2 + 3 = 5$, then our belief that $2 + 3 = 5$ counts as knowledge. From an epistemological perspective, contingent facts should be treated similarly: If it turned out that the United States do not contain fifty states, then just in this moment it has also turned out that my belief that the United States contain fifty states does not constitute knowledge. But *if* it is true that the

United States contain fifty states, then my belief that the United States contain fifty states counts as knowledge.

The moral should be this: There are, probably, limits according to our *knowledge about our knowledge*. It is possible that what we thought we know turns out not to be knowledge, or even false. The athlete that came second had a false belief: She thought that the person that came first is a woman, and she even thought that she knew this, but the person that came first was indeed a man. Everywhere in life, it is possible that those errors happen to us. But they do not actually happen everywhere. Many of the things, I assume, that we believe and that we have good reasons to believe, are indeed true. And most of those beliefs count as knowledge. Of course, there are some beliefs that we have good evidence for but that are nevertheless false. In some cases, it will turn out that we justifiably believed something that was indeed false. In some cases, perhaps, nobody will ever find out that our justified belief was indeed false. We do not know in which cases we are 'lucky' – which of our beliefs really count as knowledge – and where the surprises are hidden. But if we form our beliefs in a rather rational way, then, roughly speaking, the probability is low that many of our beliefs are false. Most of our more or less rationally formed beliefs are indeed true, even if you cannot be sure about their truth. And these many cases are cases of knowledge. We know a lot, even if we do not know which of our beliefs constitute knowledge and which not.

Whether a certain belief counts as knowledge is decided, so to speak, by the world. Because it is the world that makes something true or false: My belief that the United States contain fifty states is true only if there, in the world, there are really fifty states that belong to the U. S. However rational my belief is formed, and how many texts about the States I may have read: If the world does not contain fifty states that belong to the U. S., then my belief is false and does therefore not count as knowledge. Since we do not have a 'perfect access' to all the facts in the world, it can happen that what we thought we knew is indeed not knowledge, but false. But there is no reason to believe that this happens in *most* cases. And in the many cases where it does not happen, there we can know something.

3.4 Knowledge and Justification

Let us come back to the crucial principle that to be a belief and to be true is necessary for being knowledge (or for constituting knowledge):

[1] $Kxp \rightarrow (Bxp \ \& \ p)$

We could simplify the way of speaking and summarize that for p to count as knowledge, it is necessary that p is a *true belief*. Is it also *sufficient* that p is a true belief? Does every true belief constitute knowledge? This would mean:

[6] $(Bxp \ \& \ p) \rightarrow Kxp$

But while principle [1] is true, principle [6] is false. There are obvious cases of true beliefs that do not count as knowledge. Some Germans, I suppose, currently believe that in

July 2010, Germany is the winner of the soccer world cup. Imagine that this becomes true. Would we say that these Germans already *knew* in June that Germany would win? It would be more adequate to say that they simply believed that Germany would win, and that they were finally 'lucky' that this belief turned out to be true. There are even clearer cases. Imagine somebody is always sitting inside in the dark, and he believes every day, for no reason, that today the sun is shining. In some cases, this belief will be true. But nevertheless, 'luck' would be a more adequate description than 'knowledge'.

So being a belief and being true is not sufficient for knowledge. But *what* is sufficient for knowledge? If a belief is true: What other condition has to be satisfied such that the belief constitutes knowledge? One condition is *justifiedness*, or good reason. The man who always thinks that the sun is shining does not have any good reason for this belief. (He does not have any evidence, for example.) His belief that the sun is shining is not justified. In contrast, if he looked out of the window and saw the shining sun, then the belief would presumably be justified and, in this case, would also constitute knowledge. And my belief that the U. S. contain fifty states is also justified; I heard this from trustworthy people and read it several times. (This does not mean that everything what 'trustworthy' people say is true. But in most cases, it is.) If my belief that the U. S. contain fifty states is not only justified, but also true, then this belief constitutes knowledge. Using $J[\alpha, \beta]$ as a symbol for 'α's belief that β is justified', we can state:

[7] $Kxp \rightarrow (Bxp \ \& \ p \ \& \ Jxp)$

Two things should be noted. First, not every justified belief is true; truth and justifiedness are two different requirements. The athlete that came second was justified in believing that a woman was faster than her; she presumably had good reason to believe so. Nevertheless, she was 'unlucky' and her belief was false. Second, it should be noted that the implication in principle [7] does only go in one direction. Every case of knowledge is a case of a justified true belief, but not every justified true belief constitutes knowledge. There are some *exceptional* cases, called Gettier-cases, where a justified true belief should not be regarded as knowledge. (Gettier 1963; see also my example with the clock that shows '5 o'clock': p. 21 et seq.).

A belief can only constitute knowledge if it is true and justified. Truth has been discussed in my first chapter. What about justification? What are we justified in believing? I decided not to go into the details of this widely discussed question. But I should mention some aspects. First, there is the position called *reliabilism*, according to which a belief is justified if and only if it is produced by a reliable process. For example, our vision is usually more reliable than the worst newspaper in the country. So a belief that is formed by your vision is usually justified, while a belief that is based on the worst newspaper in the country is usually not justified.

It not should be noted, however, that the subject herself cannot be sure whether the processes that she uses are reliable or not. So according to reliabilism, justification is something *external* to the subject, the believer. The opposite position is internalism: According to the most plausible form of internalism, roughly speaking, the subject has access to the factors that make her beliefs justified or unjustified. If internalism is right, then *I can find out* whether a certain belief of mine is justified or not. (For a more detailed discussion of internalism and externalism, see Pappas 2005.)

The most convincing internalist approach that I know is *evidentialism*. According to evidentialism, a belief is justified if and only if it is adequately based on the evidence that the believer has. If and only if you have enough evidence – and not much counter-evidence – for the claim that water is H_2O, then you are justified in believing it. (Many terms are unclear here: What is 'enough evidence'? What is 'evidence'? See, for example, Conee/Feldman 2001a and 2001b. Unfortunately, clear answers are not easy to find there.)

The two approaches that I mentioned – reliabilism and evidentialism – can also be combined. You could say that a belief is justified if and only if it is based on the evidence that you have *and* produced by a reliable process. (See Goldman and Comesaña.)

Although it is not easy to decide which theory of justification is right – and whether any true theory of justification has been proposed –, most cases seem to be rather clear. Most of us are presumably justified in believing that the United States contain fifty states: We have a lot of evidence for this claim (books, teachers, etc.) and many of our sources are relatively reliable. We are also justified in believing that $2 + 3 = 5$, for similar reasons. The same is true of our belief that pure water is H_2O. All these beliefs are justified; whether they are *knowledge*, however, is another question, because they are known only if they are true, and whether they are true is decided by the world. But at least, it is good to know that the beliefs are justified.

In some other cases, the justifiedness of our beliefs is unclear. The question whether we are justified in believing that God exists, for example, is not so easy to answer. And are we justified in believing that he does *not* exist? I will say a little bit more about religious beliefs in chapter 7.

Part II: Some Candidates for Philosophical Knowledge

In Part I of the book, I answered some general questions about truth and knowledge, such as: Is every statement either true or false? Is logic a sufficient method to find truth? Is everything that we know true? What are, besides truth, other necessary conditions for knowledge? This last question is particularly important for Part II. A belief constitutes knowledge only if it is both true and justified, and a belief is justified only if we have good reasons to hold this belief (for example, if we have strong evidence for the truth of the belief). So what exactly are we justified in believing?

We are, for example, justified in believing that the United States consist of fifty states and that water is H_2O. But this is not of much philosophical interest. What are we justified in believing *in philosophy*? This is the question that Part II deals with. There are certain philosophical theses that we have good reasons for. We are justified in believing them. Therefore, these theses (or more exact: the beliefs that these theses are true) are *candidates* for knowledge, because they satisfy one important condition for knowledge: the condition of being a justified belief. One of these reasonable theses is the thesis that human beings are completely material; this is what I start with in chapter 4.

4 On Materialism and Reduction-ism

4.1 Introduction

It has been said that human beings are not completely material. Pretty much nobody would deny that human beings have a body, which is material, but some think that additionally to this body, there is a soul, which is not material (immaterial). One of the classic proponents of such a view is René Descartes.

I cannot offer a rigorous definition of 'material'. What I call 'material' is the kind of things and properties (and facts) that physics, and natural science in general, deals with. A table, a piece of skin, an electron, a human brain, the property of being wet – these are examples of something material. If there is a human soul that survives forever outside time and space, or if there is a God outside our material word, then these would be examples for something that is not material, but immaterial. I use the terms 'material' and 'physical' identically.

The position that I sketched above can be summarized this way: The human mind is not completely material. (Indeed, the position may be that the human mind is not material at all.)[18] Another position may be that human beings, including

---

[18] I could try to define the term 'human mind'; but this would be even more difficult than a definition of 'material'. Roughly, the term 'mind' refers to phenomena such as sensual experience, thoughts, emotions, wishes, and pain. Obviously, all of these

their minds, consist only of physical parts (that the things that human beings consist of are only physical things); but that some *properties* that are related to the human mind are not material. For example, it may be said that the property of being painful or the property of feeling happy are not material. Both positions – the position that the human mind itself is an immaterial thing or has immaterial parts; and the position that the human mind is material but that there are some immaterial mental properties – can be called 'dualism'. I will subsume them under the term 'dualism concerning human beings', because the underlying idea is that human beings consist of entities of two fundamentally different sorts: physical entities and immaterial entities.[19]

One opposite position is materialism (or materialist monism) concerning human beings.

> **Materialism concerning human beings** =df. All human beings, including their minds, are completely material. All mental properties are material properties.

Obviously, this is not to say that everything that exists is material. The position only states that *human beings* are completely material. In the first part of this chapter, I will quickly argue for the claim that materialism concerning human be-

---

phenomena are related to the brain. Mind and brain are closely related. (And it has been suggested that they are even identical – by Gerhard Roth in a presentation in Tübingen, Germany.)

[19] The term 'entity' is a general term for existing things and properties.

ings is true: that human minds are something completely material, and that dualism is, therefore, false.[20]

This materialist position *seems* to have a certain interesting consequence: the consequence, roughly speaking, that the human mind is reducible to physics. Because if everything that belongs to the human mind is material (physical), then it seems that physics is the science that should discover the human mind; or at least that physics *could* discover the human mind if physics were developed far enough.

The idea is not that any currently living physicist can perfectly analyze the human mind. Rather, the idea is this: Currently, when a natural scientist (say, a neurobiologist) looks at the brain of a living human being, then the scientist cannot find out what the human being exactly thinks of. But it may be thought that this problem is only due to the current imperfectness of natural science. In the long run – or in some counterfactual situation where scientists are more intelligent and machines working better – it will or could be the case that natural scientists indeed explain the human mind completely. At the moment, we need some psychologists that talk to people and develop experiments with groups of people; but in principle, everything could be explained by natural scientists that are discovering the human brain and the rest of the body in the laboratory. Because

---

[20] From now on, I will sometimes simply say 'materialism' when I mean materialism concerning human beings. Also, I will simply say 'reductionism' when I mean the thesis that psychological theories are reducible to theories of physics.

everything that belongs to human beings is material, and material entities are discovered by natural science.

The most basic science is physics; the brain, which is discovered by brain science, itself consists of molecules, atoms, electrons etc. So the more exact we work, the more it will be *physics* that is responsible for explaining the human mind. That is a short summary of this position:

> **Reductionism** =df. All theories of the human mind (all psychological theories) are reducible to theories of physics. The more natural science is developed, the more it will turn out that natural science, and finally physics, can explain the human mind.

To some people it may seem that reductionism is an obvious consequence of materialism. (It may seem to them that if nothing immaterial belongs to human beings, then it is of course natural science – finally physics – that can discover human beings, and their minds, best.) An article that suggests the truth of reductionism is Jaegwon Kim's "The Myth of Nonreductive Materialism" (1989).[21] I will instead argue

---

[21] Two things should be added. First, Kim does not say that if materialism is true, then reductionism is true. He thinks that if materialism is true, then either reductionism is true or eliminativism is true. I think that materialism is true, but neither reductionism nor eliminativism is true. Second, although I read this article two times, it did not become clear to me whether he really thinks that reductionism – *as I define it* – is true. At some points, it seemed to me that he has some other form of reductionism in mind. But we are not concerned with the question what Kim

for the claim that reductionism is probably false; that, although the human mind is completely material, natural science and physics have no chance to explain the human mind sufficiently (not even in the long run and not even in case that physics becomes better and better).

My arguments for the falsity of reductionism will perhaps not be as convincing as my simple arguments for materialism, so some doubts will remain. Furthermore, I should note that some of my thoughts are closely related to – and to some extent caused by – John Fodor's paper "Special Sciences (Or: The Disunity of Science as a Working Hypothesis)" (1974).[22] However, the way how I present the arguments will be different and, hopefully, more convincing. Furthermore, Fodor's article focuses on the notion of natural kinds (he argues that natural kinds of psychology are not natural kinds of physics), while my article does, I think, not depend on this notion.

4.2 On Materialism

Let us come to the first point (materialism). Why should materialism be regarded as true? One reason is that more and more is found out about the physical basis of the human mind; this basis is mainly the brain. The ancient Greeks did not even know where the center of our mental processes is. Some thought that it may be the Thoracic diaphragm, a

---

thinks; we are concerned with the question what's true. (Nevertheless, I will come back to Kim later.)

[22] I thank Marcel Weber, who called my attention to this article.

place next to the lungs. And the brain was supposed to be responsible for cooling the body. Later it turned out that the brain is the mental center; and medicine, biology and biological psychology find out more and more details about the physiological fundaments of, for example, our thinking processes. Neurons transport electrical signals and are connected to every part of the body. Nowadays, machines are able to detect the relevant electrical signals from the brain, they can interpret those signals and thereby, in some rather simple cases, find out what a person thinks. It is even possible to draw simple pictures without using the hands – simply by thinking, while a machine is connected to the brain.[23] So it more and more turns out that the human mind is material (physical). Because otherwise it could, presumably, not be explained how natural science and machines can analyze the human mind with this increasing success. The continuous progress that brain science makes suggests that there is no limit with regard to the extent to which the human mind is physical. Of course, one can always search for a mental phenomenon that no physiological basis has been found for yet (perhaps consciousness is an example); but based on the previous success of natural science, it should be assumed that at some point, a physiological basis of this phenomenon *will* be found. (Or the findings that already exist will even be expanded or refined.)

But there is a second rough argument for materialism that I should mention: No good alternative is ready to hand. That

---

[23] I have seen this method in the *Forum Scientiarum*, an institution that belongs to the University of Tübingen, Germany.

is, every theory on the so-called mind-body problem that is not materialistic, seems to face serious problems. Dualism is the position that human beings are partly material, but do possess some immaterial part, or at least some immaterial properties. This makes it difficult to explain psychophysical causation (and "physico-psychological causation").

Mental events (or mental states, or mental facts) cause physical events, and physical events cause mental events. The most reasonable explanation for these forms of causation is materialism: There can be causation between mental and physical events simply because both are physical events. Causation between physical events is nothing mysterious; natural science is full of explanations of this sort (indeed, this is the main business of natural science). In contrast, if dualism were true, then psychophysical causation would be causation between immaterial events and material events; and there is no obvious explanation for such a sort of causation ready to hand.[24]

---

[24] It is reasonable not only to suppose that mental events are physical events, but also that *types* of mental events are types of physical events; and that mental properties are physical properties. Such a universal materialism – in contrast to Davidson's anomalous monism – allows for reasonable explanations of psychophysical principles such as 'hunger causes a rumbling stomach'. Those principles include types of events (hunger is not a single event), and to suppose that those mental types are physical types, makes it more reasonable to understand that the mental type of event causes a physical type of event, the rumbling of the stomach. For more arguments against Davidson's position, see Kim (1989: 33-36).

An example of "physico-psychological" causation is this: When you take certain painkillers, then your pain is reduced. Painkillers are something physical, they consist of pills. How is it possible that they influence a mental state, the state of feeling pain? The most reasonable explanation is that pain itself is something physical, something material, for example the firing of C-fibers. Then there can be a scientific explanation for the influence of painkillers on pain.

An example of psychophysical causation is this: I decide to walk on the street, and so my legs indeed start to move. A mental event (my decision, or my wish) caused a physical event (the moving of my material legs). The most reasonable explanation at hand is this: My wish is itself something material. This brain state "sends" signals to the muscles of my legs, through motor neurons. Those observations can be generalized to the claim that everything mental is material; that everything mental is a subset of everything material.

To summarize the argument for materialism that I regard as most important, I note:

(1)	Physico-psychological and psycho-physical causation take place.	p
(2)	If physico-psychological and psycho-physical causation take place, then it is probable that mental events and physical events belong to the same kind of entities.	$p \rightarrow q$
(3)	Therefore, it is probable that mental	q

	events and physical events belong to the same kind of entities. (1, 2, *modus ponens*)	
(4)	If it is probable that mental events and physical events belong to the same kind of entities, then it is probable that mental events and physical events are both physical.	$q \to r$
(5)	Therefore, it is probable that mental events and physical events are both physical. (3, 4, *modus ponens*)	r
(6)	If it is probable that mental events and physical events are both physical, then it should be assumed that materialism is true.	$r \to s$
(7)	Therefore, it should be assumed that materialism is true. (5, 6, *modus ponens*)	s

Premise (4) could be questioned. One could admit that mental events and physical events seem to belong to the same kind of events; but instead of claiming that both are physical, one could claim that both are mental! The thesis that everything is mental may be called 'idealism'. It could be said that the whole world is part of a large consciousness, or that the world that we experience is constructed by thoughts (constructivism). I am not able to evaluate those positions in detail; but I should add some ideas.

One problem of constructivist theories is that we seem to have no chance to find out whether the theory is true or not. How could we find out whether everything that we experience is only a thought? To find out whether this is the case, we would need a point of view that is itself outside the constructed world. From this point of view, we could see how something constructs the experienced world. But this standpoint from above is not possible: Constructivism just says that everything that we experience is constructed, and this means that we cannot experience the construction itself. If I am in the position from which I see how the world is constructed, then the constructivist would consistently say that even this experience, the experience of the construction process, is itself constructed. And then *this* would be a thesis that I cannot evaluate. Constructivism does not seem to be a position that can be reasonably evaluated.

A popular constructivist position is this: Our brain constructs, or constitutes, the world that we experience. (Perhaps there is a real world, but what we experience is only the constructed world.) What would be the case if this were true? If this were true, then even our experience of the brain, for example the natural scientist's experience of brains in his laboratory, would be constructed; constructed by his brain. So how could he be sure that these things before him are really brains? Even the scientist's experience is constructed. All his theories are based on experiences that are constructed by his brain. His theory that human brains construct the world that they experience, would itself be problematic, because this theory depends on experiences that are themselves constructed. And how does the scientist even know that he has a brain? How does he know that there are brains? Everything that he experiences is constructed; constructed by what? He would say: constructed by his brain. But the experience of his own brain, or the experience of the data that he sees on his screen, are constructed. Perhaps everything that we experience, including our experience of brains, is indeed constructed by a computer, in a real world where no brains exist?

The constructivist, who thinks that everything we experience is constructed, cannot make any claims about reality. He cannot even claim that it is the brain that constructs something, because this would be a claim about reality. He could only say that our constructed world *looks as if* it were the brain that constructs something. I suppose that a theory that cannot say something about reality is not a philosophical theory. This is one problem that constructivism faces.

About idealism in general, I should say this: If everything, the physical things as well as the mental, are indeed mental, then how does this position differ from materialism, which states that everything is material? Both positions, idealism and materialism, claim that mental events and physical events belong to the same kind of events (this principle has been called 'monism'). And this kind of principle is interesting for our purposes: We want to know whether human beings have two different parts, or two different kinds of properties (material properties and immaterial properties), or not. And if not, then everything interesting is answered. Whether they are completely material or completely mental, should not bother us; and whether the whole world is completely material or completely mental, does perhaps not make a difference at all. We are living *in* the world and do not have to speculate about the nature of the world as a whole.

What should have become relatively clear is that human beings do not consist of two different kinds of things or properties (which would be dualism). In what follows, I will therefore assume that materialism is true, although I could not show that the opposite extreme – idealism – is false. But it seems that it does not make a difference for our purposes whether materialist monism or idealist monism is true.

One could make up an argument against materialism based on the claim that *consciousness* is something immaterial. Some or all conscious experiences have a phenomenal character: There is something that it's like to feel joy; there is something it's like to feel pain; the visual experience of red color is also accompanied by a certain phenomenal character. It could be argued that this phenomenal character of conscious experiences is immaterial. And since the phenomenal character of conscious experiences belongs to human beings, it would follow that materialism concerning human beings is false.

Why should somebody think that the phenomenal character of experiences is immaterial? The point is that phenomenal states seem to have a first-person character that material things do not have. Heat is clearly something material. If I want to explain heat, then I can explain it by the motion of molecules, etc. The explanation may be complicated, but it can be complete. What about a mental state that has a phenomenal character, for example: pain? To say that pain has a phenomenal character means that pain is (accompanied by) a certain feeling; there is something it's like to feel pain. Can there be a complete explanation of pain, as there can be a complete explanation of heat? Perhaps one can explain pain by the firing of C-fibers. But if I know that pain is the firing of C-fibers: Do I know, then, what pain is? If I never felt pain, then, it seems, even if I know that pain is the firing of C-fibers, I do not know enough to understand what pain is. I have to feel pain, I have to experience pain; otherwise, I will not have a concept of pain. In the case of heat, it seems to be different: Heat is *identical* to the motion of molecules, and so the explanation is complete, even if I do not have any experiences with heat. But the explanation of pain is not complete as long as I do not experience pain myself. This incompleteness of third-person explanations of some mental states has been called 'explanatory gap'.

One could think that the phenomenon of heat also has an explanatory gap, so that there is no philosophically relevant difference between heat and pain. To understand heat, one could claim, it is also insufficient to know that heat is the motion of molecules; you also need to experience the feeling of heat. But this view would be confused. Heat and pain are fundamentally different. The *feeling of* heat, of course, is a mental phenomenon that can only be understood if you experience it. But heat itself is not like this: There could be heat even if nobody feels it. This is what I call 'third-person character'. But there could not be pain if nobody felt it. If nobody felt pain, then there would not be pain. The phenomenal character is essential for pain; and this is what I call first-person character. As long as you only give a third-person explanation (and this is what natural science is doing), there will be something unexplained about pain. That is the explanatory gap.

The notion 'explanatory gap' has been introduced by Joseph Levine (1983), who wrote:

> "what is left unexplained by the discovery of C-fiber firing is *why pain should feel the way it does*! For there seems to be nothing about C-fiber firing which makes it naturally 'fit' the phenomenal properties of pain, any more than it would fit some other set of phenomenal properties." (357)

I would say it with these words: The C-fiber firing and all the physical processes that happen to people who feel pain, all this does not give you an understanding of pain. Because what is essential for pain is the way how pain feels. And you cannot find out how pain feels by discovering the physiological processes (the C-fiber firing, for example).

The crucial question is this: Is the 'explanatory gap' phenomenon an argument, or can it be used for an argument, against materialism? I think: No. The fact that some mental phenomena cannot entirely be explained by natural science does not show, or even suggest, that these mental phenomena are not material. The ontological question should be separated from the epistemological question. The ontological question is the question what pain is, or what the nature of pain is. The epistemological question is the question how one can gain a concept of pain, or how one can understand pain, or how pain can be explained to somebody. Everything that the 'explanatory gap' discussion contains, belongs to the epistemological question. So it may well be that the way how we gain a concept of pain is essentially different from the way how we gain a concept of heat. Or more general: The way how we gain a concept of some mental states is essentially different from the way how we gain a concept of other material phenomena. This says nothing about the ontological topic whether pain is something material. If we consider the arguments for materialism (and against dualism), then we should not give up materialism without a good reason; and the explanatory gap does not offer any good reason.

The explanatory gap shows that our epistemic access to some mental phenomena is special; it does now show anything about the nature of these mental phenomena. It is reasonable to assume this: Pain is a material phenomenon. What is essential for pain, is a certain feeling; a feeling is also something material. A subject S can gain a concept of pain (understand the nature of pain) only if S experiences pain, that is, only if S feels pain.

4.3 On Reductionism

So let us accept materialism and ask whether reductionism is true. Above, I defined reductionism this way:

Reductionism =df. All theories of the human mind (all psychological theories) are reducible to theories of physics. The more natural science is developed, the more it will turn out that natural science, and finally physics, can explain the human mind.

I already said that in my opinion, although materialism is true, reductionism is probably false. Physics cannot explain every aspect about human beings (even if physics were perfectly developed). The reason lies, again, in the fact that explanation is not an ontological business, but an epistemic business: Something is explained *to somebody*. So even if the things we explain are physical, it may be that physics (and natural science) alone cannot explain them. Because it seems that human beings have a certain nature that does not empower them to understand every phenomenon in the same way, even if the phenomena do indeed belong to the same class of phenomena (that is, physical phenomena). To some physical phenomena we have a different access than to other physical phenomena. But let us discuss matters in some more detail.

A certain type of mental events, such as pain, is not identical with a certain type of physical events. Mental states can be realized by different brain states: For example, other animals have quite different brains, but they can also feel pain; in their case, therefore, pain is realized by another physical structure. Even among human beings, there are differences. When the brain of a human being is damaged, then another part of the brain can realize mental states that were originally realized by the damaged part of the brain. This shows that there is no identity between mental events and physical events. Mental events can be realized in different physical ways (multiple realization). This was also Fodor's starting point, in his article against reductionism (1974):

> "There are no firm data for any but the grossest correspondence between types of psychological states and types of neurological states, and it is entirely possible that the nervous system of higher organisms characteristically achieves a given psychological end by a wide variety of neurological means." (105)

Multiple realization can be regarded as a fact – nowadays even more than once. How could, then, a reduction of psychology to physics be possible? Suppose that there is a psychological theory, for example, that intrinsic motivation leads to more success than extrinsic motivation. (Roughly speaking, if you do something because you really like it and you think it is important, then you are more successful than in case you do it only for some other goods, such as money.) How could such a theory *ever* be reduced to physics, or natural science in general? The theory includes the notion of 'motivation', or '*S* is motivated'. To reduce the theory to natural science, you would have to find a scientific notion for motivation; for example, you would have to formulate the brain state that realizes motivation. But there is no certain brain state that realizes motivation; different brain states are possible (multiple realization is not only metaphysically possible, but a scientific fact). Natural science cannot even *express* every mental phenomenon with physical notions.

Of course, there is no doubt that motivation is something material. In every case where somebody is intrinsically or extrinsically motivated, there is a certain brain state, or state of the body, that realizes this mental state. But there is no *certain* physical state that realizes intrinsic or extrinsic motivation.

One could think that a physical expression of psychological terms is possible by using disjunctions. Suppose that there is a psychological theory of this form:[25]

$$m1 \rightarrow b1$$

A certain mental state ($m1$), say, pain, leads to a certain behavior ($b1$). The mental state can be realized by different physical states. So one could think that $m1$ can be replaced by the disjunction ($p1 \vee p2$): The mental state can be realized by the physical state $p1$ or by the physical state $p2$.

$$(p1 \vee p2) \rightarrow b1$$

In case that there are even more possible realizations, you can add $p3$, $p4$ etc. Is this enough to reduce the psychological theory to a physical theory? Is this the pattern according to which psychology is reducible to natural science? I think we should be skeptical here.

First, the number of possible realizations $p1$, $p2$, ... may be infinite. Then nobody could ever list all of them; and this would mean that the reduction is not possible. But the thesis that there are (or could be) infinitely many realizations is problematic. Let us suppose that the number is finite. Is

---

[25] I do not think that psychological theories are ever that simple. They are much more complicated, and they all have exceptions. But this is not our topic; let us simplify matters.

reductionism *then* true? Probably not. This is because of a second problem:

The notion ($p1 \vee p2$) cannot be understood, or explained, by physics alone. Physics cannot express what $p1$ and $p2$ have in common. Because the possible realizations of a certain mental state can be physically quite different. In the case of birds, which have an extremely different brain, certain mental states (such as pain) are realized in a physically quite different way than in the case of human beings.

If psychology were reduced to physics, then we would not use the word 'pain'; we would instead use a physical description, a description that talks of neurons, brain states, at the end perhaps atoms and even smaller entities. The physical description $p1$ and the physical description $p2$ would be extremely different. What do they have in common? Why do they appear together in the same theory? The adequate answer would be this: "Both $p1$ and $p2$ realize pain"; but this is a psychological description, which is supposed to be reduced to a physical description. As soon as we give up the psychological description, we cannot explain what we talk about (what the physical states have in common).

The same problem probably occurs in the case of intrinsic motivation. I suppose that intrinsic motivation can be realized in quite different ways. We could summarize $p1$, $p2$ etc. in one group ($p1 \vee p2 \vee \dots$); but with physical descriptions alone, we could not say why we group these different physical phenomena together. It is a general problem of reduction. Suppose you want to reduce economics to physics, and so you want to find a physical expression for money. Money can be realized by bank notes, coins, even computer data. Physical vocabulary alone cannot explain what these physical things have in common, and why they should have the same or similar effects. Another vocabulary is needed, and this is economical vocabulary.[26]

A thought experiment may provide some clarity here: Suppose we know that pain can be realized by the two physical states $p1$ and $p2$. Then somebody has an injury, and a part of his brain is damaged, so that other parts realize the states that were originally realized by the damaged part. Now, pain is realized by a different state, and this new realization is observed for the first time. Here pain is realized by $p3$. But how could physics, or natural science, find out that $p3$ is pain – without using disciplines such as non-biological psychology, which have been reduced to natural science? What natural scientists can see here is that the brain of the patient sometimes shows the pattern $p3$, but this pattern is physically much different from $p1$ and $p2$. How could natural science find out that $p3$ belongs to the same group as $p1$ and $p2$? Non-biological psychology is needed here: You have, for example, to ask whether the patient feels pain now, or to look at his behavior, and then to see whether $p3$ is active in this moment. If it is, then it is reasonable to suppose that $p3$ realizes pain. The physical structure alone does not give you the answer, because the physical structure is much different from the structures that have been observed so far. This strongly suggests that reductionism is false: that psychologi-

---

[26] This example is based on Fodor (1974: 103 et seq.).

cal theories are not reducible to physical theories, even if physics were infinitely successful. Certain things in the world only make sense to us if we use psychological vocabulary.

The crucial argument against reductionism can be summarized this way:

(1)	If reductionism were true, then every psychological notion could be successfully replaced by a physical notion.	$p \rightarrow \forall x\{(Nx \ \& \ Px) \rightarrow \exists y(Ny \ \& \ Hy \ \& \ Rxy)\}$
(2)	There are psychological notions that cannot be successfully replaced by a physical notion.	$\exists x\{Nx \ \& \ Px \ \& \ \sim\exists y(Ny \ \& \ Hy \ \& \ Rxy)\}$
(3)	Therefore, it is not the case that reductionism is true. (1, 2, predicate logic)	$\sim p$ [27]

One could think that premise (2) is false, because there is a strategy to translate psychological notions into notions that only use physical vocabulary: the interpretation of mental states as functional states (functionalism). Functionalism starts with the observation that mental states can be realized

---

[27] This is the lexicon for the right column. p : Reductionism is true. $N[\alpha]$: α is a notion. $P[\alpha]$: α is psychological. $H[\alpha]$: α is physical. $R[\alpha, \beta]$: α can be successfully replaced by β.

by different physical states (multiple realization). So what is essential for mental states is not a certain physical structure. Instead, functionalists think, what is essential for mental states is a certain input-output relation. The input and the output are both physical. The mental phenomenon 'high motivation', for example, could be translated to something like 'if you give her a sheet of paper full of exercises, then she will write down her answers very fast'. (This, of course, is not completely adequate. Motivation is a much more complicated phenomenon, and an adequate functionalist description would go into much more physical details.) The general structure is this: to understand mental states as input-output relations of the form $p_i \rightarrow p_o$. If the physical state p_i is the input, then the physical state p_o will be the output (the reaction). The way how this function is realized (by which brain structure, for example), is not essential for mental states, according to functionalism. So the fact that there is multiple realization is not interesting for functionalism; the function itself, the input-output relation, is supposed to be independent of the realization. This seems to make it possible to reduce psychology to physics; we do not need disjunctions such as ($p1 \lor p2 \lor \dots$) any more. We can, it seems, replace every psychological term m by a certain physical term $p_i \rightarrow p_o$.

But this will not work; at least not so easily. Of course, one thing that may be typical for mental states is a certain input-output relation, or functional state. But it is presumably not true that mental states *are* functional states. As John Searle noted in other words,[28] to say that a mental state is nothing more than a function, is as I would say that a train is nothing more than a function such that if I start at place A, then I will arrive at place B, while A and B are both train stations. It is true that a train brings me from one station to another. This is a property of trains, but this property is not identical to the train itself. There is not only the functional state, there is also *the very train itself* (its color, its shape, the material, the heavy weight). The same is true of mental states – although there are many differences between trains and mental states, obviously. But you cannot handle the problem of multiple realization simply by not mentioning the realizations at all.

One important property of some mental states that functionalism, as I described it, does not mention, is the phenomenal character. To rejoice in watching soccer does not only mean to jump through the air whenever soccer is on TV. What is essential for joy is a characteristic feeling: the phenomenal character. This feeling is not a function. It has an existence on its own. It is far from clear how functionalism could capture the phenomenal character of mental states.

The inadequateness of the functionalist program that I sketched becomes especially obvious in the case of so-called 'inverted qualia'. Imagine that for Bryan, everything red looks as if it were green (everything red looks 'greenish' to him). And everything green looks to him as if it were red

---

[28] in *Intentionality* (1983: chapter 10 "Intentionality and the brain").

(everything green looks 'reddish' to him).[29] Nevertheless, since he can distinguish the colors red and green perfectly, because they look just as different to him as they look different to us, he reacts to both colors just as we do. The fact that green looks reddish to him and that red looks greenish to him, does not influence his functional states. (Why should it?) So if functionalism, as I described it, were right, then there would be no difference between Bryan and us with regard to color experiences. Because all that counts for functionalism are the functional states, the input-output relations. But to say that there is no mental difference between Bryan and us is false: He experiences red and green much different from us. The difference lies in the phenomenal character of the experiences, and the functionalist program that I sketched cannot capture this character. This is why I regard the functionalist program as unacceptable.

Another way of defending reductionism has been proposed by Jaegwon Kim (1989). He writes that instead of global reductions (such as the translation of a mental notion into a single physical notion), we should believe in local reductions. The idea is this: Pain can be realized by different brain states. But this is only because there are different biological species (whatever is exactly meant by 'species'). Different species realize the same mental state in different ways. As soon as we concentrate on one species, there is only one way how a mental state (pain) can be realized. So for every species, we can state a reductionist principle such as

---

[29] I leave it as an open question whether this is biologically possible. I learned that it is possible, but I will go into the details here.

$$s_i \rightarrow (m \leftrightarrow p_i)$$

Under the condition that the organism belongs to a certain species (s_i), there is a specific physical realization (p_i) of the mental state (m). Even if this is true: Would it be enough to save reductionism? No.

The goal of reductionism is to get rid of the psychological, mental vocabulary; physics should explain the mind entirely. So terms such as m would have to disappear. (If m cannot disappear, then reductionism was not successful: In this case, psychology is still needed.) So let us suppose that m disappears, just as the reductionist program wants it. Then, the formula for pain would look like this:

$$s_i \rightarrow p_i$$

There are different species $s1$, $s2$ etc., and for every species (s_i), there may be a different physical realization of pain (p_i). So we would arrive at something like this:

$$s1 \rightarrow p1$$
$$s2 \rightarrow p2$$
$$s3 \rightarrow p3$$
with $s1 \neq s2$, $s2 \neq s3$, $p1 \neq p2$, $p2 \neq p3$.

This would be the physical notion of pain. A translation would be this: Pain can be reduced to physics, because pain means 'if the species that you talk about is $s1$, then there is the physical structure $p1$; and if the species that you talk about is $s2$, then the physical structure is $p2$; and if ...'. But now, the same question arises that already arose in the case of the disjunctions ($p1 \vee p2 \vee ...$): Physics alone cannot explain what $p1$ and $p2$, for example, have in common. Why do they belong to the same group? The reason is that they all realize *pain*. But this cannot be said, if reductionism works, because the only vocabulary that the reductionist wants to use, at the end, is physical vocabulary.

For example, if we find a new species, $s4$, and we want to add the according formula ($s4 \rightarrow p_i$) to our list: How should we know which physical structure p_i is the right one for our list? Perhaps the brain of species $s4$ is much different from the brains of $s1$, $s2$ and $s3$; the physical structure that realizes $s4$'s pain is much different from $p1$, $p2$ and $p3$. With the help of physics alone, you will, therefore, not find out which physical structure should be added to the list. But if you use psychological vocabulary, then you remember that our list is a *pain* list. We talk about a certain mental phenomenon, which is pain. So the realization $p4$ that you have to add is exactly *the one physical structure that realizes pain in case of species s4*. (And if there are several structures that can realize pain in species $s4$, then add all of them.) This is what you have to search for. And it is a psychological, not a physical investigation.

I hope it has become clear why materialism is probably true and reductionism is probably false.

5 On the Question whether everything is Fluent

It has been written that the world is not separated into independent objects, or facts, but that instead everything essentially depends on other things, or even that everything depends on everything. One may go so far as to say that there are not even 'things'; the world is a whole and cannot be separated into parts, such as different things. There are no borders between one thing and another. Nothing remains the same during the time; everything is fluent. The whole is continuously changing. I call this position the 'Everything is fluent' position.

Some people may find this position appealing. Do we know that the position is true? In this chapter, I argue for the thesis that the 'Everything is fluent' position is not an example of philosophical knowledge. It may even be said that, in contrast, we know that *not* everything is fluent. Because it does not seem that there are any good reasons to think that everything is fluent.

David Bohm has explicitly argued for the view that everything is fluent, in his book *Wholeness and the Implicate Order* (1980). His arguments are related to quantum mechanics, one of the fundamental theories in current physics that especially describes the behavior of things on micro-level (atomic and sub-atomic level). How is quantum mechanics related to the idea that everything is fluent? One crucial point seems to be this: The objects that quantum mechanics describes can, according to some interpretations, not be understood as separated particles. For example, two atoms that are far away from each other seem to depend on each other; if one of them has the property 'spin 0.5', then the probability that the other one has 'spin 1.0' increases. The properties of the two atoms are correlated (Paradox of Einstein, Podolski and Rosen). Since there is no interaction between the atoms, the correlation is interpreted in this way: The atoms are not separated objects, but somehow belong together. It does not even make sense, it seems, to speak of two objects. Those findings have been generalized by David Bohm to the claim that the whole world does not consist of separated objects, but of one whole.

So far so good. But how can this show that everything is fluent? What this interpretation of quantum mechanics suggests, is that objects are not separated, not independent from each other; perhaps one could even go so far as to claim that everything somehow depends on everything. (This may or may not be an exaggeration, I don't know.) But this claim is different from the claim that everything is fluent. The claim that everything is fluent includes the position that nothing remains the same, or that nothing remains stable, during the time; that there are no objects, because after a moment, it is not the same object any more. This is a claim about the relation between objects and time. This claim should be treated seperately from the claim that objects depend on each other; *that* is a claim about the relation between objects. I suppose that quantum mechanics may provide good reasons to believe that the relation between objects is not as we used to think. But here we are not concerned with the relation between objects. We are concerned with the relation between objects and time – with the thesis that everything is fluent during the time. Is there an argument for *this* thesis?

When Bohm argues for the claim that everything is fluent (he calls this principle 'flow'), he refers to the ancient Greek philosopher Heraclitus: "The notion that reality is to be understood as process is an ancient one, going back at least to Heraclitus, who said that everything flows." (Bohm 1980: 48) He also refers to the ancient Greek philosopher Zeno (cf. p. ix). So we should try to find an argument for the 'Everything is fluent' idea there.

Interestingly, by studying the relevant positions of Heraclitus and Zeno, one will not find an argument for the 'Everything is fluent' idea at all. Heraclitus did, for all we know, not even literally write that everything is fluent (although it is often said that he wrote this). And the paradox of Zeno that Bohm refers to does not provide any argument for the thesis that everything is fluent.

Let us start with Heraclitus. The statement that everything is fluent (Greek: 'Panta rei'), cannot be found in any of the writings of Heraclitus that survived. Wilhelm Capelle explains (1968):

> "The famous simple expression 'Panta rei' is based on writings that are younger, namely by Aristotle [who interpreted Heraclitus], but Aristotle did not literally use this expression, either." (132, footnote; my translation)

94

What can indeed be found in Heraclitus' writings, are these fragments:

> "It will always flow different water to those who get into the same rivers." (Heraclitus: fragment 12; my translation)

> "We get into the same rivers, and yet we do not get into the same ones; it's us, and yet it isn't us." (fr. 49a; my translation)

I am not going to decide whether this expresses an 'Everything is fluent' position or not. It certainly sounds similar to such a position, but it does not seem to be clear. And, obviously: An *argument* for the 'Everything is fluent' position cannot be found here. Let us have a look at Zeno's paradox, which Bohm also referred to.

The famous paradox purports to show that in a race between Achilles and a turtle – where Achilles is much faster than the turtle but starts some meters behind it – Achilles can never get ahead of, or catch up with, the turtle. This is supposed to have mathematical reasons: From a mathematical point of view, it seems, there is no certain moment or place where Achilles catches up with the turtle. He comes closer and closer, that is, the distance between him and the turtle becomes smaller and smaller, without ever being exactly zero. This goes on infinitely long, since space can be divided infinitely, according to mathematics. And that looks like an example for the 'Everything is fluent' character of the world; for this reason, presumably, Bohm refers to Zeno in (1980: p. ix).

But just as there is no argument for the 'Everything is fluent' idea in Heraclitus' writings, there is no such argument in

Zeno's paradox either. First of all, the thought experiment according to which Achilles never catches up with the turtle, is not an adequate description of reality; it is rather the opposite. In reality, as we know and observe, the faster runner *will* get ahead of the slower one, and not only come closer and closer. Analogously, if Achilles existed, then he would of course get ahead of the turtle. Zeno's paradox cannot be understood as a description of reality; rather, it shows how reality *would* be if certain mathematical considerations were physically correct. Since reality is in fact not like this (the faster runner does get ahead of the slower one), we have to give up the idea that certain mathematical considerations are physically correct. Physics – which offers fundamental descriptions of reality – works differently than these simply mathematical considerations. So what Zeno's paradox may provide is something like this:

(1)	If the mathematical idea that space is fluent (infinitely divisible) were physically correct, then a fast runner could never get ahead of a slow runner.	$p \rightarrow q$
(2)	It is not the case that a fast runner can never get ahead of a slow runner.	$\sim q$
(3)	Therefore, it is not the case that the mathematical idea that space is fluent (infinitely divisible) is physically correct. (1, 2, *modus tollens*)	$\sim p$

So what Zeno actually suggested here, is that the picture according to which everything is fluent is *not* adequate. Reality does not work as this flow picture tells us. And Zeno knew that: He lived in the fifth century before Christ and was a scholar of Parmenides. Just as his teacher, Zeno believed in the opposite of an 'Everything is fluent' concept: He believed that there is no motion in the real world (compare, for example, fragment 14, in Capelle 1968: 177). To show that no motion exists, he started with the opposite position, the position that motion really exists, and tried to show how this position leads to difficulties. Those difficulties – and one of them was presumably the thought experiments including Achilles and the turtle – were interpreted by him as proofs for the rigidness (or 'un-movedness') of the existing things. But of course, Zeno's own position sounds exaggerated, and we should not discuss his theories.[30]

Now, one could think that Zeno's paradox at least shows that *according to mathematics*, everything is fluent. But even this is not the case. The idea that Achilles can never get ahead of, or catch up with, the turtle, is not only physically inadequate; it is also mathematically inadequate. This can be roughly demonstrated by such a consideration:

The idea of the paradox is this. Achilles starts behind the turtle, say, 100 meters behind it. Both start at the same time. Permanently, Achilles is 10 times as fast as the turtle. Imag-

---

[30] Just one historical note: Zeno's paradox does not occur in those fragments of Zeno that survived. It is Aristotle who mentioned Zeno's paradox: in Aristotle, *Physics* VI 9.239 b14 et seq., translated from Greek into German in Capelle (1968: 178).

ine how the race is proceeding. Suppose, Achilles has reached the point where the turtle started; he has gone the 100 meters. At this time, the turtle has already gone 10 meters, because it is 10 times slower. So now Achilles is 10 meters behind. Suppose, Achilles goes these 10 meters. Then, the turtle will have gone 1 more meter. So Achilles is 1 meter behind. As soon as he will arrive at the point where the turtle is now, the turtle will be 0.1 meters ahead. And this continuous infinitely long; the distance becomes smaller and smaller, but, it seems, there is never the moment or the place where Achilles could catch up with or get ahead of the turtle.

Let us give a slightly more rigorous description.[31] Let us calculate the distance that Achilles has to go until he catches up with the turtle. As we said, he has to go 100 meters, then again 10 meters, then 1 meter, then 0.1 meters etc. So the distance that he needs is this series:

$$100 + 10 + 1 + 0.1 + 0.01 + \ldots$$

Because as soon as he has gone 100 meters, the turtle has gone 10 more meters, which he has to go, and then the turtle will have gone 1 more meter, which he has to go, etc. The above series can also be presented in this way:

---

[31] The following discussion is based on Institut für Mathematik Paderborn (2009). Unfortunately, this page contains a mathematical mistake, which the interested reader will easily find.

$$\sum_{s=0}^{\infty}\left[100*\left(\frac{1}{10}\right)^{s}\right]$$

Written as a decimal number, you get:

111,11111111…

So this is the mathematical 'problem' in Zeno's paradox: If you write down the distance that Achilles has to go until he exactly catches up with the turtle, as a decimal number, then you need infinite space. The series of Ones (111,111…) never comes to an end. But this is only one way of presenting the distance. Above, I wrote down another presentation, the one that includes the sigma sign, and there nothing is problematic.

What will have happened, for example, when Achilles has gone 112 meters? At this time, he will definitely have got ahead of the turtle. Because 112 is greater than 111,111…, the number of meters that he needed to catch up with the turtle. So from a mathematical point of view, just as from a physical point of view, it can easily be explained how Achilles can catch up with and get ahead of the turtle. The number 111,111… is, if you use the presentation as a decimal number, infinitely long. But the number is not infinitely *great*. The number 112, for example, is greater than 111,111… And this is why Achilles can pass the turtle. The only mathematical problem related to Zeno's paradox is that the number of meters that Achilles has to go to catch up with the turtle cannot be written down as an ending decimal number.[32]

It should be concluded that neither the writings of Heraclitus nor Zeno's paradox provide any argument for the thesis that everything is fluent.

---

[32] Bohm offers another interpretation of Zeno's problem. Zeno thought that the – alleged – problem with Achilles and the turtle is a consequence of the false position that everything is fluent. Bohm, in contrast, thinks that the alleged problem with Achilles and the turtle is a consequence of the *opposite* principle: the principle that time could be divided into parts. With the help of his flow theory, Bohm thinks, Zeno's problem can be avoided. (cf. Bohm 1980: 200 et seq.) However, I think I demonstrated that there is not even any problem here. Zeno's thought experiment is not a problem to begin with. – Bohm also offers another argument for the thesis that everything is fluent: We experience music and videos not as sequences of parts, but as fluent. (chapter 7) This is an interesting psychological phenomenon, which shows something about our experience of the world. But our experience of the world is, as everybody knows, in many cases by far not identical to the real nature of the world.

6 On Utilitarianism

6.1 Introduction

So far, I gave some examples for reasonable theses in theoretical philosophy, namely in the philosophy of mind, the philosophy of science, and metaphysics. Now we can have a look at practical philosophy, namely ethics. What do we know about our moral obligations? I do not have an answer to this question. But what may indeed have the status of knowledge, is the thesis that there is one rather convincing ethical theory: utilitarianism. The plausibility of utilitarianism is the topic of this chapter.

Utilitarianism is a type of answer that has been given to the question what we ought to do (what we should do).[33] Utilitarianism is the view that you should always do what leads to the highest possible amount of utility. So if you have three options what to do, then choose the one option that leads to more utility (or equally much) than the others. Utility is not identical to money, but, for example, to happiness, or in more exact words: to the sum of happiness and unhappiness, while happiness can be expressed my a positive number and unhappiness by a negative number. An important feature of utilitarianism is the principle that you should not only consider the consequences for yourself, but also the

---

[33] I treat expressions such as '*S* ought to do', '*S* should do' and 'it is *S*'s obligation to do' as identical, although these expressions have different connotations.

consequences for all the other sentient beings that will be affected by your action.

There are several forms of utilitarianism, and I will discuss only one form, or one group of forms, the one that I regard as most convincing. I will simply say 'utilitarianism' when I speak about this form, or group of forms, of utilitarianism. Several arguments have been developed against utilitarianism, and they seem to be so obviously sound that many people regard utilitarianism as an unacceptable ethical theory. One example is Ernst Tugendhat (1993: especially 325 et seq.)[34]. An example among American philosophers is Sterling Harwood (1993). He wrote:

> "… though I reject some of the objections to utilitarianism that I still found to be worth presenting …, the remaining objections collectively have enough force to convince me and many others to reject utilitarianism." (153)

However, I argue that a closer look at utilitarianism can help to defend utilitarianism against most of the objections. Some of the arguments against utilitarianism are simply not sound. Utilitarianism is much more convincing than it seems. This will be the main thesis of this chapter. Nevertheless, some difficulties remain, as we see at the end.

Utilitarianism, as I discuss it here, has these rough features:

- Whether an act is morally right or wrong (and the degree of rightness or wrongness), depends only on the conse-

---

[34] Unfortunately, I cannot discuss the details of Tugendhat's criticism.

quences of the act. (consequentialism) If there is no possible alternative act that would presumably have had better overall consequences, then the act is morally right; otherwise, the act is morally wrong.

- Utilitarianism evaluates single actions. (act-utilitarianism) That is, nobody should accept general rules such as 'Do not lie'. It would be a mistake to claim that lying is generally morally wrong. Whether an act is morally right or wrong, depends on the consequences of just this single act – and not on the type of action that the act belongs to. There may be, for example, cases where a lie leads to overall positive effects. In such a case, lying may be morally right.

- What kind of consequences determines whether an act is morally right or wrong? Everything that counts morally are felt satisfactions and dissatisfactions. I will also speak of happiness and unhappiness, hedons and dolors. All this means the same – except for the fact that the terms 'hedons' and 'dolors' are more exact, because they can be counted. A certain act, for example, may lead to 5 hedons and 10 dolors; this means that the act will lead to twice as much unhappiness (felt dissatisfaction) as happiness (felt satisfaction). An act that leads to 5 hedons and 10 dolors is presumably morally wrong, except there is no better alternative act.

- The happiness and unhappiness that utilitarianism takes into account, is the happiness and unhappiness in the whole universe. Since not every thing in the universe is able to feel hedons and dolors (for example, joy and pain), not every being has to be considered. A stone, for example, is presumably not a sentient being; the consequences that my actions have on a stone, are not morally relevant, except the status of the stone has itself a consequence on a sentient being. The consequences that my acts have on animals that can feel pain, *are* morally relevant.[35]

We can summarize these features in this way:

Utilitarianism =df. An act is morally right if and only if its consequences lead to more (or equally much) happiness in the universe than all possible alternative acts.

Here, as I already mentioned, 'happiness' is to be understood as the sum of hedons and dolors, while hedons are positive numbers and dolors are negative numbers. For example, imagine I have the choice between two acts. The first option would make Emily slightly unhappy (1 dolor, that is: -1); the dog would not care (0); and Tim would become very happy (5). There are no consequences on other sentient organisms in the universe. (Of course, this is a simplification; there may always be some consequences.) The total amount of happiness is then:

---

[35] In my discussion, pain and suffering are treated simply as types of unhappiness, that is, as types of dissatisfaction. This does not mean that pain and suffering were just the same as our unhappiness after a lost soccer game. Of course, (heavy) pain and suffering are *extreme* cases of unhappiness. And they should be symbolized by a high-valued negative number.

$$-1 + 0 + 5 = 4$$

The other possible act is this: I simply do not do anything, which would make Emily slightly happy (1); the dog would not care (0); and Tim would become slightly unhappy (-1). The total amount of happiness would be:

$$1 + 0 - 1 = 0$$

In this case, it is my moral obligation to perform the first act, because it leads to more happiness than the second act. Similarly, if the first act led to a sum of -5 and the second possible act led to a sum of -9, then I would also have to perform the first act, because it is the comparatively better alternative.

Two things should be noted. First, again, this is only one form of utilitarianism (the version that I will consider in this chapter, and the version that I regard as most promising). So my definition of 'utilitarianism' above is actually not a definition of utilitarianism, but the definition of a certain type of utilitarianism (you could call it 'felt satisfaction act-utilitarianism'). But as I said, I am going to simplify matters and simply to speak of 'utilitarianism'. This simplification is not problematic, as long as we know that it is a simplification, and in which sense.

Second, I simplified the discussion so far in another respect, too. It is not possible for any of us to completely calculate the consequences of our acts on every sentient being in the universe. There are too many things to consider (the calculation would need much time), and there are many uncertainties: I can almost never, or indeed never, be sure about the consequences that my acts will have. So utilitarianism seems to require the impossible from us. But it is not required that we calculate the actual consequences; what we ought to do is to consider the *expected* consequences. If I am an engineer and build a house in a pretty unstable way, sell the house and then leave the country, then I can expect that the overall consequences on the happiness in the universe will be negative, although there is some possibility that nothing negative happens. Since negative consequences should be expected here, the act is presumably wrong. Nobody should invest too much time in detailed happiness-calculations. Although a more exact calculation can lead to better actions, it should also be considered that the time we need for the calculations is some kind of price that we pay. First of all, exact calculations would bother most of us and therefore reduce our own happiness – which has to be considered just as the happiness of another person. And furthermore, the more time we invest in those calculations, the less time we have left for good actions. It is obvious that a middle way is required here: Think before you act, but do not think so hard that your actions come too late.

Now, let us discuss some arguments against utilitarianism. I think that most of these arguments are not sound, and that, therefore, utilitarianism is stronger than it may seem. The arguments against utilitarianism that I mention here are mainly based on Harwood's "Eleven Objections to Utilitarianism" (1993), but my discussion is also influenced by Tugendhat (1993) and Otfried Höffe (2008: 7-51). While these writers finally reject utilitarianism, I will rather accept it as a comparatively good theory. The way how I defend utilitarianism is essentially influenced by Peter Singer's book *One World* (2002).

6.2 Some Deficient Arguments Against Utilitarianism

Arguments against utilitarianism (and probably against other moral views as well) usually have this structure: Utilitarianism has a certain consequence that we cannot accept; therefore, we reject utilitarianism. The logical principle here is *modus tollens*. If we call the "unacceptable" consequence of utilitarianism 'p', then the principle is this: If utilitarianism were true, then p. But it is not the case that p. (Because p is unacceptable.) Therefore, utilitarianism is false.

(1)	If utilitarianism were true, then p.	$u \rightarrow p$
(2)	It is not the case that p.	$\sim p$
(3)	Therefore, it is not the case that utilitarianism is true. (1, 2, *modus tollens*)	$\sim u$

Much depends on *intuitions* here. If utilitarianism has the consequence p, and we regard p as false: How do we know that p is false? This cannot entirely be found out by science; we talk about moral issues. The point is that we (or most of us) have a strong intuition that p, a consequence of utilitarianism, is false. And we accept this intuition, because we regard it as unacceptable to live without this intuition. I will not question this method; I will accept our main moral intuitions. What I will question is the first premise: The premise that utilitarianism does indeed have such a counterintuitive consequence. In many cases, it only looks as if utilitarianism has such a consequence, while it does indeed have other, much more plausible consequences.

One consequence that utilitarianism seems to have is the justifiedness of cheating and adultery, in many cases. Because according to utilitarianism, all that counts is the consequences of our acts: the happiness and unhappiness that our acts cause. Now, suppose that Martha wants to cheat on her husband. She is going to have an affair with some person, while her husband, a helpful and faithful man, is working at some other place to earn money for the family. It can be expected that the husband will never find out about the affair; Martha is very careful. Her husband will remain happy, for all we know. Then, it seems, utilitarianism has the consequence that Martha can – or even should – cheat on her husband. Because nobody will become unhappy, and she will even become a bit happier. But this consequence does not seem to be acceptable; her cheating is morally wrong. (Well, I do not know about your moral intuitions. Perhaps you think that her cheating is alright. Then I will probably not be friends with you.) The structure is this:

| (1) | If utilitarianism were true, then Martha's cheating on her husband would be morally right. | $u \rightarrow p$ |

| (2) | It is not the case that Martha's cheating on her husband is morally right. | $\sim p$ |
| (3) | Therefore, it is not the case that utilitarianism is true. (1, 2, *modus tollens*) | $\sim u$ |

But I think that we do not have to worry here: Premise (1) is not true. Utilitarianism can explain why cases of betrayal, such as Martha's case, are morally wrong. There are two reasons: First, presumably, Martha should not simply expect that the husband will not find out about the affair; even if she is careful and it can be expected that he will not find out about this certain affair, there may nevertheless be some changes in her behavior that suggest that something happened. And just this would be a consequence that probably makes him unhappy, or that could even damage the whole relationship or family. This is why utilitarianism can regard most cases of betrayal as morally wrong.

But if utilitarianism wants to be convincing, then there has to be a second reason. Because the first point – the possibility that the husband will in some way be affected by the betrayal – is intuitively not strong enough to explain the essential wrongness of Martha's behavior. Because even if we stipulate, somewhat unrealistically, that there is no chance that the husband will ever find out about the affair, it still seems to most of us that Martha's act is wrong.

The reason may be that those cases of cheating are bad not only for the one who is deceived, but *in general*. For all I know, the cheating may influence Martha's own character in a bad way; note that she will have to find excuses, she will have to lie, in case that somebody asks her what she did and where she was in these days. This has some influence on her, perhaps a bad conscious, but even if she does not have a bad conscious, her inner harmony will be damaged in the long run. (There is, for all I know, a certain type of inner harmony that only those people have who mainly behave morally correctly.) And presumably, her affair will influence the relationship in a negative way, even if the husband does not recognize why. These are reasons why utilitarianism can treat most cases of betrayal as bad: There is, at some point or other, a lot of unhappiness that cheating presumably causes in the long run.[36]

Let us discuss a second argument against utilitarianism. What determines the moral rightness or wrongness of an act, according to utilitarianism, is the sum of hedons and dolors – satisfaction and dissatisfaction – that the act causes *in the whole universe*, compared to the alternative acts. So it seems that we have to care about everybody, and even everybody to the same extent. Suppose that Jim has an ill son, and wants the best possible medical treatment for his son. Jim has a good, expensive insurance and can thereby make the doctor treat his son with this medication. But if he does this, then two other patients, who could otherwise both be

---

[36] This sounds pretty conservative, and indeed, people told me that many cases of cheating can influence the relationship in a good way. If those cases really exist, then these cases of cheating may be morally right according to utilitarianism. And this would be a plausible consequence of utilitarianism, I suppose.

saved, cannot get the medication. Time and medication are limited, and the case of Jim's son is an especially complicated one. Now, imagine that Jim cares about his own son much more than about the other two patients. He makes the doctor treat his son with the medication, so that his son is saved and the other two remain ill, perhaps even die. (This example is simple, surely simpler than every realistic case. But simple cases may be good to clarify some issues.)

According to utilitarianism, it seems, Jim's act is morally wrong: It causes a lot of suffering, or dissatisfaction (two patients cannot be treated with the medication) and less satisfaction ("only" one person, his son, is treated with the medication). The alternative act – not to make the doctor treat his son with the medication – would be bad for one person and good for two. This is why utilitarianism, it seems, would treat Jim's act as morally wrong. But intuitively, I suppose, we would be more reluctant here. Most people think that we should care about our family more than about people that we do not know. Some would say that Jim's act is neither morally right nor morally wrong. So the consequence that utilitarianism seems to have, is not convincing.[37]

| (1) | If utilitarianism were true, then Jim's behavior would be morally wrong. | $u \rightarrow p$ |
| (2) | It is not the case that Jim's behavior is morally wrong. | $\sim p$ |

---

[37] I got this example from Fred Feldman.

| (3) | Therefore, it is not the case that utilitarianism is true. (1, 2, *modus tollens*) | ~*u* |

But again, there is good reason to doubt the truth of premise (1). Utilitarianism can explain why acts that privilege family members and loved ones, such as Jim's case, are very often morally justified. This is because of the overall positive effects of close relationships between human beings. Imagine a world where everybody is "perfectly just": Everybody cares about everybody to the same extent, about family members and loved ones just as much as about the interests of colleagues, children of other families, members of other countries, etc.

First of all, this would not work very well: It is not easy for me to care about people that are far away and that I do not know, because I do not always know how to behave to help them. I do not know all of their wishes, or even most of them, and I do not know what the exact consequences of my acts on these people may be. I know loved ones, and myself, better than other people. So if I care about loved ones and myself more than about other people, then I will cause more happiness: If I want to do something positive for my sister, then I know exactly how I have to do it to cause happiness – whereas, if I want to help a person that is far away, there is a high probability that no positive effect will occur, because I do not know the situation of those people well, and I do not know whether my help will reach them. (This is not to say that we should never care about other people. Of course, we should care about every sentient being. But not about everybody *to the same extent*; we should privilege loved ones and ourselves to some extent.) Those considerations make it reasonable that according to utilitarianism, it is not the case that we must not privilege family members.

But there has to be some other reason, as well. I mentioned that we normally do not know what unknown people want, and how to help them; if this were the only explanation, then we could still not explain why Jim's behavior is acceptable. Because Jim *does* have enough information. He knows that if he sacrificed his son, then two people would be saved, which would presumably cause pretty much happiness in their families. But here is the point: A world where everybody is "perfectly just" is a pretty cold world. If everybody had to be afraid that his own family sacrifices him or her, as soon as the situation seems to require it, then the very basis of family and other close relationships would be lost. Human beings need groups that care about each other more than about people outside the group; this is a crucial psychological need. A world in which everybody is "perfectly just" would make everybody, or nearly everybody, unhappier. This is not only a general principle; we should be aware of the importance of close relationships in all of our important acts. And this is a utilitarian explanation for the fact that Jim's behavior is acceptable.

A third argument against utilitarianism comes from the famous doctor case:

> "a healthy and innocent person comes in for a checkup, but his doctor can maximize satisfaction by killing him and using

his organs to save the lives of five or more other people"
(Harwood 1993: 143).

Since utilitarianism says that the moral status of an action is
determined by the *sum* of happiness and unhappiness caused
by the act, it seems that making five people happy has more
weight than making one person unhappy or dead.[38] So it
seems that utilitarianism has the consequence that the doctor should kill one healthy person if five other people, who
need different organs, can be saved only in this way. This
would be a bad consequence, and therefore, utilitarianism
seems to fail.

(1)	If utilitarianism were true, then the doctor should kill the healthy person.	$u \rightarrow p$
(2)	It is not the case that the doctor should kill the healthy person.	$\sim p$
(3)	Therefore, it is not the case that utilitarianism is true. (1, 2, *modus tollens*)	$\sim u$

But premise (1) is probably false. First, matters are never as
simple as the thought experiment suggests. In reality, the

---

[38] I suppose that death, at least when the person that dies is young
or is killed, is comparable to unhappiness or dissatisfaction. Because death deprives a person of everything that she has, namely
her life. Furthermore, a person's death is bad for other people,
for example her or his family. It is obvious that one person's
death is, according to this consideration, not as bad as five people's death.

doctor would search for alternative ways to find organs for his patients. And if this did not work, then, still, killing the healthy patient and removing his organs would not automatically save the five ill patients. Not every organ is accepted by every body. These are just some of the considerations that cast doubt on the significance of the thought experiment.

Second, the doctor should not only consider the consequences that his act has on the six patients; he should consider *all* important consequences. And if he killed the patient to save the other five lives, then this would presumably have unpredictable and rather bad consequences on the society in general (that is, on all the people that live in the society). Imagine you would have to be afraid of going to a doctor, because you never know whether he may kill you and use your organs. This would cause a rather cold atmosphere in society; everybody can suddenly be sacrificed. I assume that most people do not want to live in such a society, and therefore, acts such as killing the healthy patient have overall negative consequences. Such an act reduces happiness. So utilitarianism can explain why it is usually morally *wrong* to kill one person just because five people could be saved in this way.

Another argument against utilitarianism comes from the idea that utilitarianism does not acknowledge fairness. Suppose, two parents can give 10 dollars two their two children, Adam and Bryan, together. They have to divide the sum into two parts. In the first case, they give 5 dollars to Adam and 5 to Bryan. In the second scenario, they give 7 to Adam and

3 to Bryan. It seems that utilitarianism cannot claim any moral difference between the two cases: in the first case, the sum of utility is 10 (because 5 + 5 = 10), and in the second case, it is also 10 (7 + 3 = 10). Since the sum of utility is everything that utilitarianism takes into consideration, is seems that utilitarianism leads to the conclusion that it does not matter which of these options the parents choose. But of course, this conclusion is false; it *does* matter whether Adam and Bryan get the same amount of money or different amounts. In most circumstances, fairness is important. If there is no relevant difference in the behavior of Adam and Bryan, then, presumably, the parents should give 5 dollars to each of them. If utilitarianism cannot acknowledge that, then it fails.

(1)	If utilitarianism were true, then fairness would be morally irrelevant.	$u \rightarrow p$
(2)	It is not the case that fairness is morally irrelevant.	$\sim p$
(3)	Therefore, it is not the case that utilitarianism is true. (1, 2, *modus tollens*)	$\sim u$

But premise (1) is not true; utilitarianism *does* acknowledge the importance of fairness. One reason is that utility – the highest good according to utilitarianism – cannot simply be identified with money. Everybody knows that the amount of money that one gets is not identical, and not proportional, to the amount of happiness that one achieves. Imagine you have an income of 2.000 dollars per month. If you suddenly get twice as much, that is 4.000 per month, then you will probably become happier; but *not much* happier. At least, this increase of income is not comparable to an analogous reduction of income: If you get 2.000 dollars less per month, that is, if you get 0 dollars instead of 2.000 per month, then you will certainly become *much* unhappier. Winning and losing are not symmetrical: Losing makes you unhappier to a greater extent than winning can make you happier. Or in more general terms: The more money you have, the less will it make you happier to get one more dollar, normally. The less money you have, the more important will it be to get one more dollar.

Let us look at Adam and Bryan from this perspective. According to the first scenario, they both get 5 dollars. We can roughly say that this corresponds to 5 hedons (5 'happiness points') each.

	money	utility (hedons)
Adam	5	5
Bryan	5	5
sum	10	10

As the simple calculation shows, the total utility will be 10. Now, let us suppose that Adam gets 7 dollars and Bryan only 3. How many hedons does Adam get? You could think that he gets 7 hedons; but this is not true. If 5 dollars correspond to 5 hedons, then 7 dollars cannot correspond to 7 hedons. We said that the more money you get, the less happiness will be added. Of course, your happiness may increase; but not that much. So let us better suppose that 7 dollars correspond to 6 hedons. This is still more than 5 hedons, but not as much as it would be if money and happiness were proportional.

And how about Bryan? He gets only 3 dollars. We said that 5 dollars correspond to 5 hedons; then, 3 dollars correspond to *less* than 3 hedons. Because compared to our reference number 5, 3 is a loss. We should better assume that Bryan only gets 2 hedons. These rough considerations lead to this pattern:

	money	utility (hedons)
Adam	7	6
Bryan	3	2
sum	10	8

The total sum of utility is 8! This is less than in the first scenario, where the total sum was 10. And this is a utilitarian explanation for the importance of fairness: The more you give up fairness, the more you will have rich people on the one hand, and poor people on the other. But to become richer does not make *much* happier. In contrast, to be poor presumably makes much unhappier; in many cases, it even leads to poverty and suffering. So the overall happiness will decrease as soon as money is not equally divided.[39] This is a utilitarian explanation for the importance of fairness.

There is also a second reason: Human beings tend to be jealous. As soon as Bryan *knows* that Adam gets more than he gets, he will become angry so that his happiness again decreases. Of course, at the same time Adam may become proud that he gets more that Bryan, so one might think that there will be a balance between jealousy and pride. But it seems obvious that jealousy has a much stronger influence on the happiness of a society than pride: If a high percentage of people regards themselves as poor, compared to other members of the society, then violence will threaten everybody in the long run. The happiness of many people, or even everybody, will decrease if fairness is neglected.

But this observation directly leads us to the next argument against utilitarianism. The utility of fairness, together with the fact that utilitarianism pledges us to care about the happiness of everybody, seem to have the consequence that most people in "rich" countries should give much of their money, probably more than thirty percent, to poor people all over the world. It seems that according to utilitarianism, where everybody is treated equally and where fairness leads to more happiness, everybody should have the same amount of money, or at least a comparable amount of money. Many people around the world have less than one dollar per day;

---

[39] Obviously, everything that I said here is simpler than reality. Indeed, it is sometimes said that people in poor countries are in average even happier than people in rich countries. Those phenomena need special analyses.

many others have more than fifty dollars per day. Even if all of these people who have more than fifty dollars per day gave thirty percent, that is, fifteen dollars, to poor people, then there would still be a huge difference between rich and poor. These suggestions are, of course, simplified; but the crucial idea is clear: If it is a consequence of utilitarianism that drastic inequality should be avoided, then it is also a consequence of utilitarianism that most of us should donate more than thirty percent of their income.[40] And this is intuitively exaggerated.

(1)	If utilitarianism were true, then most of us would have to donate more than thirty percent of their income.	$u \rightarrow p$
(2)	It is not the case that most of us have to donate more than thirty percent of their income.	$\sim p$
(3)	Therefore, it is not the case that utilitarianism is true. (1, 2, *modus tollens*)	$\sim u$

You may think that premise (2) is false: that we do indeed have to donate so much money. But let us assume that this requirement would indeed be exaggerated. Then, still, there is no problem for utilitarianism, because premise (1) is highly problematic. Utilitarianism does probably not have

---

[40] When I say "most of us", then I mean most of the people that live in so-called "rich" or first-world countries.

the consequence that most of us have a moral obligation to donate more than thirty percent of their money.

Suppose, to simplify matters, that there is a country A where everybody has 50 dollars per day; and another country B where everybody, or most people, have 1 dollar per day. In this case, from a simple utilitarian point of view, it is morally required that those from country A give something to those from country B, because country B is poor. Imagine, those from A give 10 dollars per day, that is, twenty percent of their income, to the people of B. If both countries have equally many inhabitants, then the new status will be this: People from A have 40 dollars each, people from B have 11 dollars each. This is a good decision; poverty in country B will be significantly reduced or even overcome, which presumably leads to more happiness (or in better words: to *less suffering*), while the difference in country A is not that significant. Whether you have 50 dollars or 40 dollars is not such a big deal; you will perhaps be unhappy that you cannot fly to Spain any more, but you will get used to it.

But to take much more steps forward, would be exaggerated. Assume that you go further, and people from A give so much money to B that both have equally much. That is, they give not only 10 dollars, but 24.50 dollars per day, so that people in both countries have 25.50 dollars per day. This would be a drastic change for country A: People would have to change their life-style significantly, and the whole structure of the country, its culture, its infra-structure, the products and apartments that are offered on the market, would have to change. And what about country B? Of course, some will be happy to have more money, that is, to have 25.50 dollars instead of 11 dollars. But the former change from 1 dollar per day to 11 dollars per day has already eliminated poorness; compared to this important step, the new change from 11 dollars to 25.50 dollars does not have such a great influence on the happiness of the people. Some will use the money to live in their own apartment for the first time in their life, and this will also lead to some loneliness. This is not to say that it would be *bad* for country B to have 25.50 dollars per day and person; but at least, it would not be much better than having 11 dollars.

Now, if you compare the situation of country A, which changes from 40 dollars to 25.50 dollars, with the situation of country B, which changes from 11 dollars to 25.50 dollars, then it is very reasonable that the disadvantages for A are more significant than the advantages for B. If you considered the sum of utility that resulted from such an operation, then you would probably come to the result that you would better not do it.

To summarize these points: Giving money from rich to poor people is presumably good, because the victory over poverty is a goal that should be aimed for by everybody who is in a position to help; and many people in rich countries could give some money, say, twenty percent of their income, without becoming as poor as people in so-called third-world countries. (Fortunately, some already do this.) But to exaggerate this principle, that is, to postulate that everybody should give money until rich and poor people have equally much, this would be a mistake from a utilitarian view. Because this second, exaggerated step, will reduce more utility than it will create.

Except for these philosophical and psychological reasons, there are also obvious political and economical considerations that raise similar doubts. It is highly controversial whether giving money to poor countries has an overall positive effect. It is clear that in case of a catastrophe or war, we have to help. But *permanent* help has disadvantages, even if the money is not abused and really reaches the people that it was supposed to reach. One reason is that stable wealth is only possible if the economical power increases in the poor country itself. In contrast, to transport the economical power of another country into the poor country, is not a sustainable solution; it may even be counterproductive, because it reduces the autonomy of people in those countries. Helping people to help themselves, supporting the development of markets in poor countries, is presumably more useful than shifting money. We should conclude that a utilitarian, who aims for a reduction of unhappiness (suffering), does not donate thirty percent of his money. He rather gives a smaller amount of money and helps in other, more intelligent ways, if he can.

6.3 Open Questions and Problems

So far, I explained why certain seeming problems of utilitarianism are indeed no problems. Utilitarianism does *not* support adultery and cheating; it does *not* force us to treat our loved ones in the same way as others; it does *not* force the doctor to kill an innocent, healthy person for the sake of saving five ill people; utilitarianism *does* acknowledge fairness as an important good; and it does *not* have the consequence that we should give so much money to others that everybody finally has the same. Now, I will mention some points that are not that clear.

If utilitarianism is true, then how would we have to change our behavior toward non-human animals, such as pigs, cows, chicken and fish? Many people eat some or all of these animals, and this is the reason why many of them have to die – and furthermore, many animals are treated in a shameful way, for example in big farms. Utilitarianism aims for as much happiness as possible, and as little unhappiness, or suffering, as possible. Certainly, eating meat makes most human beings happy; but is this happiness comparable to the amount of suffering that occurs in many cases through the shameful living in farms and the slaughtering?[41]

Those questions are not easy to answer, because some further questions arise. Are non-human animals capable of feeling pain? Presumably yes, but: to what extent? Is their unhappiness, or suffering, comparable to the unhappiness or suffering of human beings? Furthermore, how much pain does occur in the case of slaughtering? And also: If everybody stops eating meat, what dissatisfaction does arise *then*?

---

[41] Note that these are two different points: One point is the bad treatment of animals in some farms, and another point is the death of animals. Is the second point alone – death – something bad? As I already suggested, I think unnatural death is indeed a form of dissatisfaction (usually). See also Thomas Nagel's chapter on death (1979).

For example, how serious would the economical consequences be?

I do not have any good answers. However, it seems obvious that if utilitarianism is true, then mankind's behavior toward animals does have to change. At least, it does not seem to be justified that animals are treated shamefully in farms. Meat that has been produced under those unworthy circumstances should better not be consumed, because otherwise those shameful methods are supported and will not end. And *perhaps* animals should not be slaughtered at all.

Let us now mention a huge problem of the utilitarian principle. To repeat the principle, it is this:

> **Utilitarianism** =df. An act is morally right if and only if its consequences lead to more (or equally much) happiness in the universe than all possible alternative acts.

Happiness has here to be understood as the sum of satisfaction and dissatisfaction, while satisfaction counts as a positive number and dissatisfaction as a negative number. For example, think of the situation in which the United States were during the last years of World War Two. They had to decide whether they would attack Germany or not. Both options clearly would have led to significant amounts of dissatisfaction (suffering). To attack Germany had the consequence of much suffering especially among German citizens; not to attack Germany would have made these German citizens happier (at least for the moment), but it would have led to much greater dissatisfaction among other countries, which were attacked by Germany. From a utilitarian perspective, the amount of dissatisfaction should be compared; clearly, it was right to attack Germany, because the alternative (not to attack Germany) would have led to more suffering.[42]

But are there any *amounts* of satisfaction (or happiness, or suffering)? Can those kinds of goods be compared, just as numbers can be compared? For example, is it right to say that the death of four people is better than the death of five people? Is it right to say that the suffering of one million people is better than the suffering of five million people? Utilitarianism presupposes that those questions can be answered with Yes, and this is problematic.

On the one hand, I think that *some* comparison between amounts of dissatisfaction is possible. The suffering of five people is clearly worse than the suffering of four people (and this implies that the suffering of four people is better than the suffering of five people, although this sounds rude). In every-day life, we always assume – implicitly – that those comparisons are legitimate. We send soldiers to wars although we know that some of them will die. Because we think that the wealth and security of the population at home have more weight than the lives of some soldiers, although this is a hard decision. We accept some deaths to avoid more deaths among the civilians. The war against terrorism costs lives, but if we did not risk those lives, then – many people think – terrorist attacks will lead to even more deaths. It is

---

[42] This is not to say that *the way how* they attacked Germany was morally perfect.

those comparisons that lead to many of our decisions. And there is nothing generally wrong about that.

Note also this example that Harwood gives (1993):

> "For example, we build freeways even though we know that it is just a matter of time before an innocent baby who would not have died nearly so soon had the freeway never been built gets crushed in an automobile accident on the freeway. But the great convenience of the freeway and the other lives saved by allowing ambulances and other emergency vehicles to use the new freeway to speed to emergencies outweighs the harm caused to the crushed baby." (151 et seq.)

These are implicit comparisons between amounts of dissatisfaction and satisfaction. We all accept it, it's just that we do not explicitly mention them, because the comparisons are hidden in the complexity of normal life and its causal relations. Utilitarianism just makes those considerations *explicit*. It explicitly suggests that amounts of dissatisfaction and satisfaction should be compared to come to a good decision. This honesty is rather an advantage than a disadvantage of utilitarianism.

On the other hand, a good decision according to utilitarianism will sometimes require precise calculations. We would have to attribute numbers to certain amounts of satisfaction or dissatisfaction. Is this possible? It is clear, for example, that cancer is worse than ten minutes of pain in a leg; and it is clear that losing a loved one is worse than losing five dollars (at least for most people). But how could somebody find adequate numbers? If -3 is the number for pain in a leg, then what is the number for cancer? -100? -1000? This seems arbitrary and inadequate. And it does not help to describe the situation in more detail, for example, to describe the type of cancer, the duration and intensity of pain, etc. Still, it does not seem that any certain number is adequate. This is an essential problem of utilitarianism, and I do not know a solution. What I hope is that numbers are not necessary for utilitarian considerations; that we can come to a good decision even if we do not attribute numbers.

Another problem concerns the relation between satisfactions and dissatisfactions. Sometimes, we have to compare amounts of happiness with amounts of unhappiness to come to a decision. Above, I gave the example of Emily, the dog and Tim: A certain act would make Emily slightly unhappy (-1), the dog would not care (0) and Tim would become pretty happy (5). The total sum is 4, so that the act is morally right (given that there is no alternative act that would be even better). But is it possible to treat satisfaction and dissatisfaction as simple opposites, as something symmetrical to each other? Utilitarianism presupposes that this is possible. But such a principle is problematic:

Suppose that dolors (that is, amounts of dissatisfaction) are simply the negations of hedons (amounts of satisfaction), just as utilitarianism assumes. Then, the following would be true. I have a permanent pain in my feed for one month, because of an accident. The pain is not very extensive, say, 1 dolor (that is, -1 hedons). In the afternoon, I read some nice pages written by Albert Camus (1 hedon). What is my status while reading Camus? I have the pain in my feed, and at the same time I enjoy Camus. So the total status is supposed to be $-1 + 1 = 0$. The sum is simply 0. If this were true, then my happiness while reading Camus would be the same as my happiness while doing nothing without any pain! This seems wrong. When I do not have pain and do not read Camus, then my feeling is presumably *neutral*. But having pleasure and pain at the same time is not neutral. It is different.

Pain does not simply outweigh pleasure, and pleasure does not simply outweigh pain. Rather, it seems that these are two fundamentally different phenomena. Utilitarianism presupposes that an act that makes one person happy and one person unhappy is morally equivalent to an act that does not make anybody happy or unhappy at all. But these are two fundamentally different cases. Utilitarianism seems to be based on a false theory about human beings.[43] It seems to me that this is an unsolved problem of utilitarianism, and I do not know how serious the problem is and whether it can be solved.

6.4 Conclusions

In this chapter, I discussed a certain ethical theory, which could be called 'felt satisfaction act-utilitarianism'. This theory, just as utilitarianism in general, seems to have a lot of problems, as many philosophical writings suggest. But indeed, a closer look at utilitarianism shows that many of these problems do not exist. Most consequences of utilitarianism are convincing. The thesis that utilitarianism rightly answers to the question what we should do, is a good candidate for

---

[43] These considerations are based on Fred Feldman's lectures.

knowledge in practical philosophy. However, some questions remain open.

For example, it seems that if utilitarianism is true, then the way how many human beings treat non-human animals – especially their consumption of meat – cannot be morally justified. If this is true, then *either* utilitarianism *or* mankind's behavior toward animals has to be given up (or both). Another open question concerns the countability of satisfaction; it is not clear how satisfaction and dissatisfaction could be expressed by numbers. And the fact that utilitarianism treats satisfaction and dissatisfactions simply as opposites, such as positive and negative numbers, is threatened by serious counterexamples.

However, it can be supposed that every theory is confronted with open questions and difficulties. *If* there can be any true ethical theory at all, then utilitarianism is a rather convincing and good candidate.[44]

---

[44] The conditional clause is important here: the question whether there is any true ethical position, cannot easily be answered with Yes. One should also be aware of this problem: If no human being has a choice about her actions (that is, if there is no Free Will), which is probable, then we can never choose between any alternative acts. We always have exactly one option! What is, then, the advantage of any ethical theory that tells us which alternative act is better? This does not seem to have any significance if we do not have alternatives to begin with. But this is a deep question, too deep for me.

7 What do we Know about Free Will and the Existence of God?

7.1 Introduction

Free Will and religion – two of the most important and interesting topics – are going to be discussed together in one chapter. This is not because I wanted to discuss the *relation* between Free Will and religion, such as the question whether Free Will is possible given that an omnipotent God exists. (For this question, see Pike 2010 and Boethius 2010.) However, at one point we will say something about the relation between Free Will and religious beliefs, namely at the point where we discuss an argument against the existence of God (the so-called Argument from Evil).

Throughout the rest of this chapter, I will treat Free Will and God as two different topics. They are joined together in one chapter mainly because they share one important feature: The answer to the question whether human beings have a free will, and the answer to the question whether God exists, both essentially depend on your definitions (the definition of 'Free Will' and the definition of 'God'), and there does not seem to be any agreement with regard to the question how these terms should be defined. Especially the notion of God is extremely unclear, as the plurality of religious views shows. I would not feel comfortable if I gave exactly one definition of 'Free Will', or exactly one definition of 'God'. And so I cannot answer to the question whether we are justified in believing that Free Will exists, nor whether we are justified in believing that God does not exist. But I will propose certain definitions and say what we probably know about Free Will *if* these definitions are accepted.

7.2 Free Will

The term 'free will' is misleading; discussions about Free Will in philosophy are indeed not discussions about the question whether our will is free (for example, whether we have a choice about our wishes). Discussions about Free Will are rather discussions about *actions*: Do we have a choice about what we do? Or: Can we do what we want? Is there any act of any human being that is performed freely? Whenever I write 'Free Will', in capital letters, then I refer to questions of this sort, questions that concern our freedom with regard to our actions.

Let me explain one possible definition of 'Free Will'. Nobody thinks that we have infinitely many possible options how we could act. Our freedom is limited. For example, I am certainly not able to fly through the air without any machines. I am probably not able to concentrate on a hard topic for twenty hours without a break; my inner forces are not strong enough. And I am not able to become the president of the United States, because these guys don't let me. So the question is not whether we have infinitely many choices; obviously we have not. The question is, in contrast, whether anyone of us has *any* choices. For example, I am sitting here at my desk. It seems that I have a choice about that; that I could also do something different. For example, it seems that I have some alternatives ready to hand, I could choose walking in the sunset instead of sitting here. But some philosophers, going back to Ancient Greece, have claimed that we never have any choices. If this is what we want to discuss – and I think that this is indeed what most philosophers discuss in their texts about Free Will –, then we should define 'Free Will' this way:

> **Free Will** =df. the thesis that at least one human being has a choice about at least one of her actions. 'Having a choice' means: being able to do something else than what one actually does.

If this is the definition of 'Free Will' that you choose, then it should most likely be concluded that there is no Free Will. The crucial point is Peter van Inwagen's "Consequence Argument", although this argument has to be refined in different ways. Van Inwagen's argument can be found in his book (1983: especially 94 et seq.). It can be summarized and interpreted as follows.

Suppose that determinism is true. That is, suppose that our universe is governed by laws of nature (that is, basic physical laws) that determine exactly one possible future.[45] From one state of the universe in the past together with our laws of nature, a certain future follows with necessity. Human beings are completely material (compare my chapter 4). So if everything material is determined, then human beings are

---

[45] Classic candidates for the laws of nature are Newton's physical laws. Nowadays, the theories of relativity are a better candidate, and also the quantum theory, which leads to some difficulties.

also determined. Now, how should Free Will be possible? Nobody has a choice about the past; the past is just as it was. Nobody has a choice about the laws of nature, either. We have to accept them. And we do not have a choice about the conjunction of both. These claims can be symbolized by

$$N(P \& L),$$

where N means 'nobody has a choice about', that is, 'nobody could do something such that not ...'.[46] P is a proposition that expresses the complete state of the universe at a time in the past. And L is a conjunction of the laws of nature.[47] We have assumed that determinism is true; so we have assumed that the conjunction $P \& L$ entails a certain future, including every act of a human being. Let us use the symbol A for any act of human being. For every act A, A is entailed by $P \& L$, the past and the laws of nature. According to the laws of nature, there was only one possibility when and where we were born; what our genes would be; how we would grow up; what would happen to us, and whom we would meet; what would happen in our brain; finally, how we would decide just in this case, such as my decision to sit in front of the desk instead of walking in the sunset.

---

[46] In this discussion, when I say 'nobody', this is supposed to mean 'no human being'.

[47] I follow Finch and Warfield with regard to these definitions (1998: 516).

$$(P \& L) \rightarrow A$$

And nobody had a choice about determinism. So the principle according to which every action is entailed by the past and the laws of nature, is itself something that nobody has a choice about:

$$N\{(P \& L) \rightarrow A\}$$

Now these considerations can be combined to an argument against Free Will, with the conclusion that nobody has a choice about any act:

Consequence Argument

(1) $N(P \& L)$
(2) $N\{(P \& L) \rightarrow A\}$
(3) Therefore, $N(A)$

I think that there is no relevant mistake in this argument. The argument shows that nobody has a choice about any act, and if this is what the Free Will thesis negates, then there is no Free Will. However, it should be noted that the above argument is not perfect, it has to be refined. First of all, there is a logical problem, which I will only sketch briefly. The argument presupposes, as van Inwagen sees (1983: 94), the truth of this inference rule:

$$\{N(p) \& N(p \rightarrow q)\} \rightarrow N(q)$$

But this inference rule is false, as for example Erik Carlson showed. (2002)[48] However, this should not worry us, since an improved version of the Consequence Argument exists that does not depend on the false inference rule. This improved version has been developed by Alicia Finch and Ted A. Warfield (1998: especially 522). The N-operator in premise (2) is replaced by the necessity operator $\square$. So it is not only supposed that nobody has a choice about the fact that the past and the laws of nature entail our actions; but that our actions are a *necessary* consequence of the past and the laws of nature. This is a reasonable consequence of determinism: Given the past and the laws of nature, it was and is *not possible* that I decided to have a walk; it is necessary that I sit here.

Improved Consequence Argument

(1) $N(P \& L)$
(2) $\square\{(P \& L) \rightarrow A\}$
(3) Therefore, $N(A)$

This argument is valid. So if you do not like the conclusion that we never have a choice about our actions (that there is no Free Will), then you should say which of the premises is false in your opinion, and why. I think that this is not going to be successful.

---

[48] It should be noted that Carlson does not explicitly argue against the Consequence Argument, but against another argument, the Mind Argument. But Carlson's argument is indeed a general argument against the above inference rule.

David Lewis rejects premise (1) of the argument, in "Are we Free to Break the Laws?" (1981). He thinks that in a certain sense, we can change the laws of nature, such that other actions could have been performed! So in a certain sense, I could have changed the laws of nature in a way that would have made it possible for me to have a walk instead of sitting in front of my desk. Of course, Lewis does not say this literally: He does not say that we can *cause* a change of the laws of nature. But, he suggests, we could do something such that were we to do it, then other laws of nature would be actual. He gives the example of raising his hand: He does not raise his hand, but, he claims, he could have done it.

> "Had I raised my hand, a law would have been broken beforehand. The course of events would have diverged from the actual course of events a little while before I raised my hand, and at the point of divergence there would have been a law-breaking event – a divergence miracle ... But this divergence miracle would not have been caused by my raising my hand. If anything, the causation would have been the other way around." (125)

I would call this view *mysterious*. It says that divergence miracles are possible, that is, events that are contradictory to our laws of nature such that if these events take place, then other things happen than those which happen according to the actual laws of nature. Free Will is supposed to be possible because those divergence miracles are possible. How this is going to work – I do not know. It does not seem plausible to me that anybody can change the laws of nature, in any way.

There is another argument against the Improved Consequence Argument: One could claim that premise (2), the thesis of determinism, is false. Because according to standard interpretations of current physics, the laws of nature do not determine a certain future. They only make certain future states *more probable*. This position has been called 'indeterminism'. Let us suppose that indeterminism is true (this is indeed plausible). Then, premise (2) in the Improved Consequence Argument fails; and the argument as a whole fails. But what happens? It remains true that there are laws of nature in our world – presumably those laws that quantum theory includes. The fact that these laws are not deterministic, is due to the fact that the behavior of particles on quantum level (atomic and sub-atomic level) is not predictable; there is some amount of pure *chance*. It has been claimed that the existence of this pure chance can be mathematically proven. So far so good. But how is this going to save Free Will? It remains true that there are laws of nature, and that we do not have a choice about them; it remains true that we cannot change the past; and now we know that there are random quantum mechanical events, as well. But do we have a choice about *them*? No, presumably we do not have a choice about those events either! They are random, and not caused by our conscious mind.

Perhaps it is possible to formalize these considerations.[49] The Consequence Argument was based on the idea that the past state of the universe together with the laws of nature determine our actions. This does not seem to be correct any more. Today we assume that the past state and the laws together are not enough to determine the future; there are still different possible actions, because different quantum mechanical events may take place. If somebody wanted to predict our future actions – which is of course not realistic, and not even possible – then it would not be enough to know the state of the universe at a certain time and the laws of nature; he would also have to know what the outcomes of all relevant random quantum mechanical events will be (for example, which atom will have spin 0.5 and which will have spin 1.0). *If* he could also know these quantum mechanical results, then he could predict the future.

So why should we not simply add the outcomes of all relevant random quantum mechanical events (say, Q) to our list? The past state P of the universe at some time $t1$ together with the laws of nature N together with the outcomes of all random quantum mechanical events between $t1$ and the time when the act A is performed, determine the act. And this is true of all acts. (premise 2 below) And we do not have a choice about these factors. It is highly plausible that

---

[49] The argument against Free Will that I am developing here is new, for all I know. It is essentially different from an already existing argument for the incompatibility of Free Will and indeterminism: the Mind Argument. The Mind Argument is probably not convincing. See, for example, Graham (forthcoming).

we do not have a choice about the past and the laws of nature and the outcomes of random quantum mechanical events. (premise 1)

Consequence Argument for Indeterminism

(1) $N(P \& L \& Q)$
(2) $\Box\{(P \& L \& Q) \to A\}$
(3) Therefore, $N(A)$

This is a presentation of the simple idea that the indeterminism in our world does not provide any reason to think that there is Free Will. If there is no Free Will in a deterministic world – which has been demonstrated by the Improved Consequence Argument – then there is no Free Will in our world either, because the only difference between a deterministic world and our world are random events, which are random, and therefore not something that we could have a choice about.

But obviously, all this depends on the definition of 'Free Will' that we gave above. We said that to have a free will means to have about a choice about one's actions. I regard this definition as the most common one. But the definition has one disadvantage: If we define Free Will as having a choice about actions, then Free Will is not directly related to ethics. But some people think that Free Will *should* be directly related to ethics, and that our definition should therefore be given up. The point is that according to our definition, which identifies Free Will with having a choice, it is possible not to act freely but nevertheless to be morally responsible. This is a somewhat counterintuitive outcome;

some of us want to say that if your act was not performed freely, then you are not responsible for this act (it was not your free decision!). But if you want such a close connection between Free Will and moral responsibility, then you need another definition of Free Will, not the one that identifies Free Will with having choices.

How is it possible not to have a choice about one's act but nevertheless to be morally responsible for this act? This is what Harry G. Frankfurt showed in his (1969) paper. Instead of repeating his famous, but rather unrealistic example (cf. especially 835 et seq.), I give this example of a similar sort. Suppose that nobody has a choice about any of her actions, just as I argued in the previous paragraphs (given our definition of 'Free Will', nobody is free). It seems that there are still some differences with regard to the moral responsibility that we have for our acts. Compare Tommy and me, who both perform the same kind of act. We both kiss a woman that is not identical to one of our wives. I do it just because I want to do it. (Of course, I do not have a choice about it, because I do not have a choice about anything. But it is also true that I *want* to do it. This is my wish, and I do not have a choice about this wish, either.) Tommy, in contrast, kisses the woman only because he is forced by other people. He is an actor and has to kiss her in front of the camera; the director suddenly told him to kiss her, and if he refused to do it, then he would lose his job. Tommy does not *want* to kiss her. He wished he could escape the whole dilemma. Now, it is reasonable to say that I am morally responsible for the act of kissing the woman, while Tommy is not. Or at least: that there is some difference with regard to our moral responsibility. And this is true although we both do not have a choice about the act, since nobody has a choice about anything![50]

You may think that a definition of Free Will should somehow capture this difference; that a definition of Free Will should have the outcome that I kiss the woman freely and Tommy not. Because I am morally responsible and he is not. Then, we need another definition of Free Will – one that does not require choices, a requirement that nobody meets anyway. You could now give this definition, which has indeed been suggested in a presentation:[51]

> **Free Will** =df. a subject's ability to perform an act that this subject *wants* to perform

According to this definition, many or all of us have a free will in many circumstances. My act of sitting here is an example of Free Will, because I want to sit here and simply do it. The drinker who opens a beer is perhaps not that free; but when most of us open their beer at a party, then this is an example of Free Will. Tommy was not free when he kissed that woman, because there was some nearly irresisti-

---

[50] You can find more serious examples. For example, compare two people who do something morally problematic in their job, but while one of them does it because he simply wants to do it, the other one feels some pressure because he would otherwise lose the job and endanger his family. You may say that both are morally responsible – but certainly not to the same extent.

[51] Gerhard Roth, Tübingen, Germany. Unfortunately, I do not remember the exact words that he used.

ble external pressure; but I was free when I kissed her. The new definition of Free Will makes it possible to find Free Will at many places. The previous definition did not allow for any Free Will among human beings. This shows how much depends on your definition here. (And both definitions are acceptable.)

7.3 The Existence of God

The relation between philosophy and God is problematic. In chapter 2, I already said that in philosophy usually only arguments count. The existence of God, and perhaps the non-existence of God as well, do not seem to be phenomena that you could find arguments for. So why should a philosophical book even talk about this issue? This is because people have actually thought that they could demonstrate God's existence or non-existence with arguments. One person that thought he could sufficiently argue for the existence of God is Anselm of Canterbury (2010): "You exist so truly, O Lord my God, that you cannot be thought not to exist." (170) A person that thought he could sufficiently argue against God's existence is David Lewis (e. g. 2007). But I do not think that we know that God exists; the famous arguments for his existence are not promising. Do we know that he does *not* exist? Whether an argument against God's existence is promising, depends on the definition of 'God'.

Let us start with arguments for God's existence. Before I discuss one of them in slightly more detail, I should mention two other arguments for his existence that have been given.

One is the Cosmological Argument, which has roughly this structure:

(1)	Everything that exists is caused by something else.[52]	p
(2)	If everything that exists is caused by something else, then there is some first cause.	$p \rightarrow q$
(3)	Therefore, there is some first cause. (1, 2, *modus ponens*)	q

The idea is that the chain of causation cannot go back for-ever. At some point, there must have been something that started the chain. But it is not clear why premise (2) should be accepted. Why should the chain not go back to the past forever? Or it may be a circle structure: A causes B, B causes C, C causes A … You may think that all this is implausible, and therefore accept the argument. But then you should notice that the argument is not even enough to demonstrate that God exists. The conclusion of the argument is that some first cause exists (or existed). This first cause may be some physical event. Why should it be God? The Cosmo-logical Argument should not be regarded as an argument for the existence of God – this has also been suggested by Peter

---

[52] The term 'everything that exists' does not refer to God itself. Otherwise, premise (1) would claim that God is itself caused by something else, which is not the idea.

van Inwagen in his chapter on the Cosmological Argument (1993: p. 210, footnote 2).

Another argument for the existence of God is the Teleological Argument. Its several versions could perhaps be summarized this way:

(1)	Some things in nature are designed for certain purposes.	p
(2)	If some things in nature are designed for certain purposes, then there is an intelligent designer who created these things (God).	$p \rightarrow q$
(3)	Therefore, there is an intelligent designer who created these things (God). (1, 2, *modus ponens*)	q

Such an argument – with more details – can be found in Paley (2010). The point is that the human eye, for example, seems to have a certain purpose: It should help us to see something. It seems that the eye is *made* for vision. This can be generalized to the claim in premise (1). And if the eye is made for some purpose, then there has to be somebody who made it. And this is supposed to be God, as premise (2) says.

But I suppose that the theory of evolution gives more convincing explanations. Some things *look as if* there were designed. To say that they are designed for purposes, as premise (1) wants it, is problematic. I would rather say that the processes of evolution led to the current result that we have such an eye. But even if you want to accept the claim that our eye, for example, has a design and a purpose, that is, if you want to accept premise (1), then you should not accept premise (2). The "designer" of our eye is not a person, but the process of evolution. (This is not to say that God does not exist. But the fact that some things in nature look as if they were designed, does not provide any reason to think that God exists. If there are reasons to think that God exists, then these reasons must be somewhere else.)

The most interesting argument for God's existence is, I suppose, the Ontological Argument. Van Inwagen presents it in this way: (1993)

> "If we look within ourselves, we find that we possess the concept of a perfect being. ... But existence itself is a perfection, since a thing is better if it exists than if it does not exist. But then a perfect being has to *exist*; it simply wouldn't be perfect if it didn't. ... Just as three-sidedness is a part of the concept of a triangle – the mind cannot conceive of triangularity without also conceiving of three-sidedness – existence is a part of the concept of a perfect being." (76; italics in the original)

Later, van Inwagen replaces 'existence' by the property 'necessary existence' (cf. 77 et seq.), but these details should not bother us at the moment. The idea is this: Imagine the greatest possible being, a perfect being, as van Inwagen says. (Which is identical to God.) Now imagine that this greatest possible being does *not* exist. Then, it would not be the greatest possible being: Because now you could imagine

146

something that is even greater, namely, a greatest possible being *that exists.*

Existence is itself a perfection. Something that does not have the property of existence, is never the greatest possible being, because it is possible that there is a greatest possible being that indeed exists, and this one would be greater than the one that does not exist. These considerations can be summarized this way:[53]

(1)	A perfect being (God) has all perfections.	$\forall x \{ Gx \rightarrow \forall y (Py \rightarrow Hxy)\}$
(2)	Necessary existence is a perfection.	Pn
(3)	Therefore, a perfect being (God) has necessary existence. (1, 2, *predicate logic*)	$\forall x \{ Gx \rightarrow Hxn \}$

But as van Inwagen points out, this argument does not provide any reason to think that a perfect being exists! Premise (1) is, in more exact words, the claim that 'Everything that is a perfect being (God) has all perfections', or in still more exact words, 'For all x, if x is a perfect being (God), then x has all perfections'. But this does not answer the question whether there *is* any x. It is reasonable, of course, that *if* there is a perfect being, then this being has all perfections,

---

[53] I add the right column only for people who are interested in formal logic. This is the lexicon. $G[\alpha]$: α is a perfect being. $P[\alpha]$: α is a perfection. $H[\alpha, \beta]$: α has β. n : necessary existence.

including necessary existence. But this does not answer the question whether there is a perfect being or not. It belongs to the concept of a greatest possible being that it exists; but this does not answer the question whether the concept is realized. *If* it is realized, then there is a greatest possible being that exists. Whether it is realized or not, is still an open question.

What the Ontological Argument actually does, is this: It uses the inexactness of our language. When we hear a sentence such as 'A perfect being (God) has necessary existence' (conclusion 3), then we are inclined to think that this implies that there is a perfect being. But this inclination is deceiving. The conclusion only says that 'Everything that is a perfect being (God) has necessary existence'; this is indeed what the argument shows. The question whether the term 'everything that is a perfect being (God)' refers to anything existent or not, is still another question.

We can conclude that the Ontological Argument is not a convincing argument for God's existence.[54] It does not seem that there is any convincing argument for God's existence ready to hand. And this is no surprise; there may be good reasons to believe in God's existence, but those reasons cannot have the form of arguments. Religious reasons are not philosophical reasons.

It has been said that philosophy can show the opposite, namely, that God does *not* exist. I decided to focus on a certain argument against God's existence, that is the Argument

---

[54] For a more detailed discussion, see again van Inwagen's chapter on the Ontological Argument in (1993).

from Evil.[55] The Argument from Evil starts with the observation that there is a vast amount of evil in the world. If there were a God, then he would not allow that much evil. Because God is supposed to be omnibenevolent and omnipotent, that is, he is morally perfect and can do everything. If he existed, then it would not be possible that he wants so much evil to happen, or that he is unable to remove this evil. (Perhaps God would allow *some* evil to happen, because he may want us to enjoy good moments more than we would enjoy them if there were no bad moments. But he would never allow that much evil that we actually recognize. Many people suffered and suffer a lot in their lives, without any compensation during their lifetime. Think of Auschwitz or of extreme poverty, illness, and violence. A God would not allow such evil. So we should conclude that he does not exist.)

| (1) | There is a vast amount of evil in the world. | q |
| (2) | If God existed, then there would not | $p \rightarrow \sim q$ |

---

[55] One other argument against the existence of God focuses on the notion of omnipotence. Those who believe in God presumably believe in God's omnipotence. But omnipotence, according to this argument against God's existence, is not a consistent concept. Can an omnipotent being create a stone that is too heavy for him to lift? However you answer this question, it seems to follow that the omnipotent being is *not* omnipotent, which is a contradiction. But this seeming problem in the notion of omnipotence can be solved: cf. Harry G. Frankfurt (1964).

	be a vast amount of evil in the world.	
(3)	Therefore, it is not the case that God exists. (1, 2, *modus tollens*)	~p

This argument may or may not be convincing, I am not sure. Peter van Inwagen argued that the argument is problematic; he questions the truth of premise (2). It may well be that God exists and that he allows that much evil to happen, for complicated reasons. The main thought can be summarized as follows. (cf. van Inwagen 2006: 85 et seq.) The evils that happen in the world are a consequence of the Free Will that human beings have. God gave us Free Will, because Free Will is so good that its goodness outweighs the evils that result from it (or from the abuse of Free Will).

But why did Free Will cause so much evil? According to the story, human beings were originally living in harmony with God and without Free Will; they were, so to speak, governed by him but also protected by him. They had paranormal abilities that saved them from all evils, even from earthquakes and the like. Then, God gave rationality and Free Will to them, because, as we said, Free Will is an important good. It is a necessary condition for *love*. When they had gained Free Will, the human beings decided – for some reason – to divide themselves from God. The free decision to be divided from God had the implication that human beings became the victims of chance (for example, victims of conflicts, earthquakes and other evils).

It was not possible for God to give Free Will to the human beings *and* to determine what they would decide; this would not have been Free Will, van Inwagen thinks (see, e. g., 72 above: "To ask God to give me a free choice between x and y and to see to it that I choose x instead of y is to ask God to bring about the intrinsically impossible"). Since the human beings have divided themselves from God, he has a plan: He wants that human beings love him, cooperate with him and be re-united with him. This plan can only work if human beings experience a lot of evil. Otherwise they would not know what it means to be divided from God, and so they would not cooperate with him. This is why God does not remove (many of) the evils that are caused by people's Free Will.

You may or may not find this story realistic. The most urgent problem of such a story is, in my opinion, that it depends on the existence of Free Will. Does Free Will – the kind of Free Will that is presupposed in the story – exist? I do not know. Perhaps we should not make a decision and conclude that it remains an open question whether God may exist.

But there is another Argument from Evil, as well. This Argument focuses on the evils that happen in hell. It was developed by David Lewis, and it has been written after his death on the basis of some of his notes (2007). People that go to hell stay there infinitely long; so the amount of evil that happens to them is infinitely large. This is not fair: Whatever they did in their life-time, this was not *infinitely* bad. Everything in life has limits, but hell doesn't. So the notion of God is inconsistent: On the one hand, God is supposed to be omnibenevolent (morally perfect), and on the other hand, he is supposed to be responsible for this unfairness in hell. This is inconsistent, and we should conclude that God does not exist.

The problem of this argument is that it depends on the notion of hell and on God's omnibenevolence. Perhaps there is no hell? If you take some religious books, such as the bible and the Qur'an, *literally*, then you may think that the existence of God is inevitably combined with the existence of hell. But there are other forms of theism, and many people do not literally believe in religious books. God may exist without having the property of sending people to hell.

Or perhaps God is not omnibenevolent? Why should there not be a notion of God that does not include the property of moral perfection? Lewis' argument against God's existence does not apply to those religious views. Much, or even everything, depends on your definition of 'God' here. And it does not seem that one definition is better than the other one.

Bibliography

Adler, Mortimer J., 1985: *Ten Philosophical Mistakes*. New York.

Anselm of Canterbury, 2010: "The Classical Ontological Argument." In: Basinger et al., eds.: 169-170.

Basinger, David, William Hasker, Michael Peterson and Bruce Reichenbach, eds., 2010: *Philosophy of Religion*. 4th edition, Oxford.

Boethius, 2010: "God Is Timeless." In: Basinger et al., eds.: 150-152.

Bohm, David, 1980: *Wholeness and the implicate order*. London.

Capelle, Wilhelm, 1968: *Die Vorsokratiker. Die Fragmente und Quellenberichte*, translated and introduced by Wilhelm Capelle, Stuttgart.

Carlson, Erik, 2002: "In Defence of the Mind Argument." *Philosophia* 29 (1-4): 393-400.

Comesaña, Juan, forthcoming: "Evidentialist Reliabilism".

Conee, Earl, and Richard Feldman, 2001a: "Evidentialism." In: Hilary Kornblith, ed.: *Epistemology. Internalism and Externalism*, Oxford 2001: 82-107.

– 2001b: "Internalism Defended." In: Hilary Kornblith, ed.: *Epistemology. Internalism and Externalism*, Oxford 2001: 231-260.

Deutsch, David, 1996: "Comment on Lockwood." *British Journal for the Philosophy of Science* 47 (1996): 222-8.

Deutsche Bibelgesellschaft, 2002: *Die Bibel*. Translation Martin Luther, Stuttgart.

Diezemann, Gregor, 2006: "Physikalische Chemie II/Quantenmechanik." http://www.uni-mainz.de/FB/Chemie/AG-Theoretische/index-Dateien/Page3893.html

Engesser, Kurt, Dov M. Gabbay and Daniel Lehmann, 2007: *A New Approach To Quantum Logic*. College Publications.

Evers, Dirk and Niels Weidtmann, eds., 2009: *Wahrnehmung und Identität. Ich, Flow, Lügen, Raum, Kulturelles Gedächtnis*, Berlin.

Finch, Alicia and Ted A. Warfield, 1998: "The Mind Argument and Libertarianism." *Mind* Vol. 107.427: 515-528.

Fodor, Jerry A., 1974: "Special Sciences (Or: The Disunity of Science as a Working Hypothesis)". *Synthese* 28 (1974): 97-115.

Frankfurt, Harry G., 1964: "The Logic of Omnipotence." *Philosophical Review* 73.2 (1964): 262-263.

– 1969: "Alternate Possibilities and Moral Responsibility." *Journal of Philosophy*, 66/23 (1969): 829-39.

Gettier, Edmund, 1963: "Is Justified True Belief Knowledge." *Analysis* 23 (1963): 121-123.

Goldman, Alvin, forthcoming: "Toward a Synthesis of Reliabilism and Evidentialism? Or: Evidentialism's Troubles, Reliabilism's Rescue Package."

Graham, Peter, forthcoming: "Against the Mind Argument."

Hardegree, Gary, 2010: "Derivations in Identity Logic." http://people.umass.edu/gmhwww/310/pdf/unit4.pdf

Harwood, Sterling, 1993: "Eleven Objections to Utilitarianism." In: Louis Pojman, ed.: *Moral Philosophy. A Reader*, Indianapolis: 141-154.

Höffe, Otfried, 2008: *Einführung in die utilitaristische Ethik*. 4th edition, Tübingen.

Hofmann, Frank, 2008: *Die Metaphysik der Tatsachen*. Paderborn.

Institut für Mathematik Paderborn, 2009: "Zenons Paradoxon von Achill und der Schildkröte." http://math-www.uni-paderborn.de/~mathkit/Inhalte/Reihen/data/manifest0/einstieg.html

Inwagen, Peter van, 1983: *An Essay on Free Will*. Oxford.

– 1993: *Metaphysics*. Boulder/CO.

– 2006: *The Problem of Evil*. Oxford.

Lewis, David, 1981: "Are we Free to Break the Laws?" *Theoria*, 47 (1981): 112-121.

– 2007: "Divine Evil". In: Louise Anthony (ed.): *Philosophers Without Gods*. Oxford: 231–242.

Kant, Immanuel, 1787/1956: *Kritik der reinen Vernunft*. 2 volumes, ed. Wilhelm Weischedel, Frankfurt/M.

Kim, Jaegwon, 1989: "The Myth of Non-reductive Materialism." *Proceedings and Addresses of the American Philosophical Association*, Vol. 63, No. 3. (Nov. 1989): 31-47.

Levine, Joseph, 1983: "Materialism and Qualia. The Explanatory Gap." *Pacific Philosophical Quarterly* 64 (1983): 354-361.

Nagel, Thomas, 1979: "Death." In: id.: *Mortal Questions*. Cambridge: 1-10.

Paley, William, 2010: "The Analogical Teleological Argument." In: Basinger et al., eds.: 212-214.

Pappas, George, 2005: "Internalist vs. Externalist Conceptions of Epistemic Justification." Stanford Encyclopedia of Philosophy, http://plato.stanford.edu/entries/justep-intext/

Pike, Nelson, 2010: "Divine Omniscience and Voluntary Action." In: Basinger et al., eds.: 144-149.

Popper, Karl R., 1934/1994: *Logik der Forschung*. 10th edition, Tübingen.

Ratzinger, Joseph Kardinal, 2005: *Werte in Zeiten des Umbruchs. Die Herausforderungen der Zukunft bestehen*, Freiburg i. Br.

Searle, John R., 1983: *Intentionality. An Essay in the Philosophy of Mind*, Cambridge.

Singer, Peter, 2002: *One World. The Ethics of Globalization*, 2nd edition, New Haven.

Sweet, Dennis, 1995: *Heraclitus. Translation and Analysis*, Lanham.

Thomas Aquinas, 2010: "The Classical Cosmological Argument" (originally: "Summa Contra Gentiles"). In: Basinger et al., eds.: 184-186.

Tugendhat, Ernst, 1993: *Vorlesungen über Ethik*. Frankfurt/M.

Williamson, Timothy, 2007: *The Philosophy of Philosophy*. Oxford.